PAPER TIGERS
AND
MINOTAURS

D1365433

A CARNEGIE ENDOWMENT BOOK

PAPER TIGERS AND MINOTAURS:
THE POLITICS OF VENEZUELA'S ECONOMIC REFORMS

MOISÉS NAIM

A CARNEGIE ENDOWMENT BOOK

Copyright © 1993 by The Carnegie Endowment for International Peace, 2400 N Street, N.W., Washington, D.C. 20037

Distributed by The Brookings Institution, Department 029, Washington, DC, 20042, USA. 1/800-275-1447.

Copy editor: Rebecca Krafft
Cover: Supon Design Group

Library of Congress Cataloging-in-Publication Data

Naim, Moises
    Paper Tigers and Minotaurs: The Politics of Venezuela's Economic Reforms/Moises Naim
    p. cm.
    Includes index.
    ISBN: 0-87003-025-6: $24.95.—ISBN: 0-87003-026-4 (pbk): $8.95
    1. Venezuela—Economic policy. 2. Venezuela—Economic conditions—1958-
3. Venezuela—Politics and government—1975-
    I. Title. HC237.N35 1992
    338.987—dc20   92-35295
                                                          CIP

The Carnegie Endowment for International Peace

The Carnegie Endowment was founded in 1910 by Andrew Carnegie to promote international peace and understanding. To that end the Endowment conducts programs of research, discussion, publication, and education in international affairs and American foreign policy. The Endowment also publishes the quarterly journal, *Foreign Policy*.

As a tax-exempt operating foundation, the Endowment maintains a professional staff of Senior and Resident Associates who bring to their work substantial firsthand experience in foreign affairs. Through writing, public and media appearances, congressional testimony, participation in conferences, and other activities, the staff engages the major policy issues of the day in ways that reach both expert and general audiences. Accordingly the Endowment seeks to provide a hospitable umbrella under which responsible analysis and debate may be conducted, and it encourages Associates to write and speak freely on the subjects of their work. The Endowment convenes special policy forums and, from time to time, issues reports of commissions or study groups.

The Endowment normally does not take institutional positions on public policy issues. It supports its activities principally from its own resources, supplemented by governmental and philanthropic grants.

To Susana

Contents

List of Tables and Figures

Figures

Tables

Foreword

The management of market reforms is perhaps the principal public issue in more and more countries, from the old socialist ones to the diverse economies of Latin America. Venezuela is a particularly interesting subject of study in this regard because, unlike so many other countries undergoing reforms, it had so many more things going for it but still ran into big trouble. This study of Venezuela's experience with far-reaching change provides an insider's look at the real problems governments have to contend with in managing the transformation of their economies. It focuses on the political economics of change, and makes clear inter alia some basic considerations that are too often dismissed in today's disdain of government—that effective market reform requires a strong state and that an adequate flow of public information is essential to the success of radical economic measures. The Venezuelan experience has a relevance for all reformers: the quality of governance is crucial to success.

Few are as well-equipped to provide this searching and broad examination as Moisés Naim. He is scholar, management specialist, and economist. Most important he was a Venezuelan cabinet minister deeply involved in the development process, with a principal responsibility for Venezuela's liberalization program. His experience as an executive director of the World Bank enabled him to inject into his analysis a useful comparative perspective. Naim has brought to this work not only superb technical capabilities but a deep commitment to the public weal and to successful market reform as a necessary concomitant to the growth of democratic stability.

Economic reform is reshaping much of the world and international relations. It is a subject of much interest to the Carnegie Endowment and affects many of its programs, including its new efforts in the former Soviet Union. The Endowment is pleased to present this important study of the reform process. The views expressed are, of course, the responsibility of the author alone.

Morton Abramowitz
President
Carnegie Endowment for
International Peace
Washington, D.C.

Introduction

Jeffrey Sachs

Moisés Naim has written a brilliant book about the ongoing struggle for economic reform. His penetrating analysis in fact goes far beyond Venezuela and helps uncover the common contours of the economic reform process around the world. In countries as seemingly diverse as Venezuela, Poland, and Russia, there are deep similarities in the tumultuous process of creating market-based, democratic societies after decades of state control and weak or nonexistent democratic institutions. This book should be required reading for the dozens of presidents and finance ministers around the world now engaged in this effort, though Naim's narrative makes painfully clear why these reformers have so little time for reading and reflection on the job: an overwhelming amount of their time and energy must be devoted simply to holding hard-won terrain and dodging political, and sometimes real, bullets.

Naim is a member of the select group of modern-day scholar-politicians leading the battle for economic and political modernization throughout Latin America, Eastern Europe, and the former Soviet Union. As a distinguished Venezuelan academician deeply versed in political and economic science, Naim was tapped by President Carlos Andrés Pérez at the beginning of 1989 to be Venezuela's minister of industry, with the mandate to liberalize and modernize Venezuela's international trading system. Naim successfully led the process of deregulating the economy and of opening Venezuela's markets to

Galen L. Stone Professor of International Trade at Harvard University and economic advisor to governments in Latin America, Eastern Europe, and the former Soviet Union. Professor Sachs advised the government of Venezuela in 1989 on behalf of the United Nations Development Program.

foreign trade and investment, and he has the battle scars to show for it. Readers can be thankful that he eventually withdrew from day-to-day politics to gain the time to reflect deeply on the political process.

The book is actually three in one. It is a trenchant account of a bankrupt state in which failed political and economic institutions imploded after decades of corrosion, corruption, and encrustation. Second, it is a very wise assessment of the practical possibilities and limitations of economic reform. Naim explains why certain measures must be implemented with shock therapy, while other parts of the reform will require years or decades for improvement. Finally, it is an invaluable guidebook for future reformers, explaining how politics is likely to evolve in the face of reforms and suggesting certain areas to which scarce attention and energies can usefully be directed by the political leaders of the reforms.

The Bankrupt State

Naim vividly and perceptively conveys the central point of the 1989 Venezuelan reforms. They were not merely a mid-course correction of the economic dials, but were nothing short of a fundamental response to state bankruptcy. Again and again, Naim underscores the calamitous condition of the Venezuelan state by the end of 1988, when Carlos Andrés Pérez won the presidential election. In purely financial terms, the state was insolvent. Foreign reserves were depleted; the international debt could not be paid. The financial collapse had created the conditions for hyperinflation to emerge, though price increases were temporarily repressed by artificial price controls. As in Eastern Europe and the former Soviet Union at the same time, shortages of basic commodities intensified under the weight of large budget deficits, price controls, and widespread hoarding in anticipation of impending price increases.

Naim takes great pains to demonstrate that the financial insolvency was only the monetary aspect of a deeper insolvency, reflecting the collapse of Venezuela's postwar political-economic model. Although Venezuela had been a democracy since 1958, Naim explains that the political parties and major corporatist interests in the society (such as the trade unions and employer federations), had increasingly failed to "aggregate" social interests in a truly pluralistic and democratic manner. Increasingly, they had become the leading participants in a feeding frenzy in which privileged groups plundered the dwindling resources of the ever-weakening state. Venezuela's oil wealth no doubt encouraged the plunder by contributing to the widespread perception held by Venezuelans and foreign creditors alike that the country remained rich despite the ostentatious levels of influence peddling, patronage, and capital flight in the 1970s and 1980s. A similar delusion about oil wealth had diverted attention from Mexico's grave institutional weaknesses in the late 1970s.

By extension, Naim's analysis sheds considerable light on the collapse of the communist state. By trying to manage all aspects of economic life the communist regimes like the Venezuelan state found themselves hostage to powerful interest groups—in the regions, the military-industrial complex, and the state farms—and these groups ended up destroying the state by plundering public finances. Lacking popular legitimacy, the communist regime had no basis of support except among the very groups that were decimating its capacity to operate. While the situation took a long time to unravel, with oil and foreign borrowing delaying the collapse (as in Venezuela), state insolvency ended the communist regimes just as it brought down Venezuela's postwar political-economic model, and at practically the same time.

The Reform Program

Naim describes incisively the lack of any real choice between "shock therapy" and "gradualism" in a time of profound crisis. At the start of 1989, the Venezuelan government simply lacked the financial means, the autonomy of operation, and the administrative capacity to move gradually in areas of macroeconomic stabilization, trade reform, and price liberalization. The true alternative to "shock therapy" would have been a combination of hyperinflation, extreme shortages, and collapse of the basic supply system. The macroeconomic outcome after 1989 certainly justified the approach the government took. Venezuela turned within two years from a situation of economic decline, depleted reserves, shortages, and imminent hyperinflation to one of growth, reserve accumulation, and substantial, though incomplete, price stabilization.

In fact, shock therapy is not solely an economic strategy but also a fundamental political strategy. By attempting to extend its limited capabilities to all aspects of the economy, the Venezuelan state lost the capacity to deliver even the *core* domestic functions of government: monetary stability, contract enforcement, public order, and a basic social safety net. In resorting to the shock therapy approach the government retreats from inessential tasks, so that it has a chance to meet its core responsibilities. It is, in the end, a political strategy for restoring a viable state.

One of Naim's most important themes, however, is that certain microeconomic reforms simply cannot be carried out as rapidly as the macroeconomic reforms. This is not a plea for gradualism in macroeconomic measures, and still less in the microeconomic ones. Naim is rather emphasizing the *inherent* stresses that arise because certain reforms take a very long time to bring to fruition. The most striking and politically damaging lags in Venezuela have come in the delivery of social services, such as education and health. Already in ruins by 1989, these social services will remain in disrepair for years to come at great social cost and political risk to the government.

Once again, Naim's analysis sheds light on events in the postcommunist societies. From afar, shock therapy in Poland and Russia has often been challenged as unnecessarily traumatic. Critics, however, have failed to gauge the scope of the financial and institutional crisis left behind by the *ancien regime* and the resulting absence of practical alternatives to rapid and deep measures, as in Venezuela. Outside observers have sometimes naively called upon the dispirited, politicized, incompetent, and often corrupt bureaucracy inherited from the communist state to implant a highly nuanced market-oriented reform program based on an optimal, gradual design. Of course, the bureaucracy has no training in or affection for a market economy, and much of it prefers to fight a rear-guard action of antimarket measures aimed at assuring its self-preservation and the continuation of privileges and powers of the old system.

Political Management

The great paradox of the Venezuelan experience is that significant macroeconomic accomplishments—rapid GNP growth, circumvention of hyperinflation, promotion of exports—have been accompanied by profound political turmoil, including two coup attempts. One shudders to think what macroeconomic failure would have produced! One of the great strengths of this book is the author's clear explanations of the reasons for this seeming contradiction.

At the start, Venezuelan society was not prepared for the shock. In the eyes of its citizens, Venezuela was still rich, even if the elites were skimming the profits on their own account. The overt signs of collapse had been suppressed by the Lusinchi government through 1988. Rather than adjust to reality, the Lusinchi administration chose to deplete the country's foreign reserves, leaving an empty coffer for the next government. Even less prepared than the general public, it seems, were the old guard of the Venezuelan corporatist state, including political leaders of the major parties and the private businessmen favored by the system of subsidies and state protection.

As Naim makes plain, the new government too was unprepared at the political level, even if it was better prepared at the economic level. The team of young technocrats, the author among them, knew what to do economically, but they had few defenses prepared for the social upheaval that came soon after. They were likewise ill-equipped for the trench warfare that has ensued since 1989 as the elites of the old system, including even the congressional leaders of the governing party, have fought as viciously as the Russian *nomenklatura* to maintain their privileges and power even as the old system is reduced to rubble.

Naim is surely right that the government lost opportunities by failing to communicate with the public better. It played the old politics among the corporatist leaders, while a new and broader-based politics was needed. But Naim concedes, at least implicitly, that there were limits to what could be communicated. The public was surprised and angered by the measures in 1989, and afterwards the party hacks of the old system were desperate and well positioned to slow, if not defeat, the reforms.

In the end, Venezuela will need a new politics to integrate with its new economics. The two coup attempts almost led to a new politics of a harrowing and deadly sort. Naim puts his hopes in a further democratization of the society to match the radical restructuring of the economy. New political forces, including those given a voice by the democratization of local and state governments, are less beholden to the special interests of the old system. Interestingly, despite the deep political animosity for President Pérez and the reform government, Venezuelans elected many backers of economic reform in the state elections held in late 1992. The optimistic but plausible view is that the public is venting its rage at the old guard rather than at the reform process itself.

At first glance, it might seem ironic that reforms in Poland have progressed with less political turmoil than in Venezuela. Venezuela, after all, was much closer to a market economy and democracy; its economic crisis was less severe; and its macroeconomic results since the start of reform have been superior. Naim's analysis helps us understand the somewhat steadier progress in Poland. There the old guard was substantially pushed aside after the 1989 revolution. The authors of the failed system were seen as illegitimate lackeys of the Soviet authorities. A new class of politicians, many rooted in the Solidarity opposition movement, rose to power in national and local elections. Even the old *nomenklatura* in industry was substantially replaced by new young managers supported by Solidarity-led workers' councils in the state-owned factories. Part of President Pérez's problems, in contrast to Walesa's is that despite leading remarkable reforms, Pérez remains inextricably linked in the public's mind with the old and discredited system, having been Venezuela's dominant political figure in the 1970s.

The situation in Russia is closer to that of Venezuela than is Poland's. As of early 1993, the old political leaders had preserved many of their traditional power bases from which they could try to stifle Yeltsin's reforms or at least to steer them to their personal and political advantage. Democratization of local government has not yet taken place, and the communist *apparatchiks* have kept a tight grip on their position in Russia's anachronistic People's Congress.

Conclusions

One's first impression upon reading this important study is to marvel at the political bravery and steadfastness of the reformers, and second is to groan at their seemingly impossible task. But in fact, the narrative gives quiet but strong grounds to take heart. While Venezuela is still in a harrowing passage between systems, the public shows signs, if grudgingly, of actually supporting the passage. Venezuelans did not rally behind the two coup attempts, even though they heaped scorn on President Pérez. They are participating in the democratic process and indeed giving a mandate to new young leaders intent on a new economy. In the final analysis, Naim's faith is properly put: first in the economic reforms which are doing their job, if not at the speed demanded by the public, and second in the public itself. Both underlie his belief that an open political system, supported by free discussion and debate, will most reliably lead Venezuela to a political and economic revitalization. Naim's book will play an important role in that revitalization and will provide instruction and support for reformers throughout the world.

Chapter 1
Paradoxes of Economic Reform

Early in 1992, Venezuelan President Carlos Andrés Pérez spoke to a large gathering of international businessmen and government officials in Switzerland. In his speech, Pérez confirmed the growing perception that Venezuela was becoming an interesting success story among countries that had broken with their interventionist pasts and were adopting market-oriented economic policies.

Pérez offered all manner of good news, showing that painful transitions toward free markets pay off and that a democratic regime can indeed survive the unpopular decisions required to bring about a more competitive economic environment in a developing country. He backed these claims with hard evidence. In 1991, not only had inflation and unemployment declined for a second consecutive year, but the Venezuelan economy had experienced one of the highest growth rates in the world. Institutional reforms were continuing apace, and the first sales in the privatization process had been internationally acclaimed for their effectiveness and transparency. Only two years after having been cut off from international credit markets, Venezuela now enjoyed the renewed confidence of both lenders and investors. In fact, international credit rating services had just upgraded the country's rating, and assessments of investment climates ranked Venezuela at the top of their world lists and, together with Mexico and Chile, as one of the preferred investment locations in the region.[1]

The following evening, just after returning to Caracas from his successful international tour, President Pérez had to run for his life as rebel army units bombed his residence and the presidential palace in an attempt to overthrow his government. While the coup failed, it galvanized the widespread resentment against Pérez and his government that had been mounting since the onset of reforms. Hardly nine months later, in November 1992, factions within the armed forces again tried, and failed, to overthrow the government. Finally, in May 1993, Pérez's government succumbed to charges of corruption and a new cabinet, less interested in reforms, was appointed.

Venezuela's extreme experience with economic reform and its political consequences offers several lessons about the nature of the transition to a market economy. While an explicitly socialist model of government had never been adopted, state ownership of the main sources of hard currency—oil, iron ore, and aluminum—and a long-standing commitment to economic nationalism and industrialization based on import substitution had created an economic system in which public agencies, not markets, were the main actors.

When the Pérez government broke with this state-centered scheme in February 1989, it was able to do so under much better conditions than most other countries attempting such changes. Vene-zuela had been a happy anomaly in a region plagued by military dictatorships, economic debacles, and political turmoil. It boasted one of the oldest democracies in Latin America, and its huge oil revenues made it prosperous and politically stable. Oil provided a reliable and sizable income that gave the government more room for maneuver than reforming countries usually enjoy. When the reforms were launched in 1989, the government had just been elected and the presi-dent was one the most popular figures in the country. Dissatisfaction with previous administrations and a decade of economic decay was widespread. The Pérez administration and its new policies were enthu-siastically and effectively supported by governments of developed countries, multilateral institutions, and the international financial com-munity. Not even two years later, however, Pérez had become one of the most unpopular presidents ever, and his government was widely rejected. Not only the survival of his government but even that of democracy had become doubtful, and the long-term sustainability of the reforms was uncertain.

Carlos Andrés Pérez had been president of Venezuela in a previous era, during the 1970s, when oil prices quadrupled and Venezuelans' living standards and expectations boomed. In 1989, however, Pérez launched a series of radical market-oriented reforms in response to changed circumstances and the dire international and economic realities the country now faced. But these reforms were grossly out of step with popular expectations fed by decades of pervasive state intervention subsidized by oil exports. Three weeks after the inauguration, in February 1989, the most violent riots in decades erupted, triggered by an increase in bus fares. That same year the country experienced its highest inflation ever as well as the largest drop in economic activity. The government stayed the reform course and kept pushing ahead with policy changes on almost every front.

In some respects, these changes paid off rapidly. During 1989, huge macroeconomic distortions were corrected, and in 1990 the economy began to grow at impressive rates. By 1991 economic growth was 10.5 percent, and in 1992—despite political turmoil and low prices for its main exports—Venezuela's economy grew by 7.3 percent, making it one of the fastest growing economies in the world. Since the onset of reforms, social safety nets for the poor were put in place, and stock market prices boomed, as did foreign investment and new exports. Inefficient and money-losing state-owned enterprises were successfully privatized, and the country's huge debt with international banks was renegotiated under more favorable conditions. Unemployment declined at a fast pace and inflation declined as well, albeit at a much slower one. Political and administrative powers were decentralized from the capital to the states. Direct elections for state governors and mayors were held for the first time in Venezuelan history in 1989.

At the same time, however, hostility, frustration, and a sense of outrage toward politicians and public officials took hold of the country. The outcomes that so pleased government officials, the International

Monetary Fund (IMF), the World Bank, and foreign investors mattered very little to average Venezuelans. Frequent public protests in 1991 were the preamble to two army revolts during 1992 that let loose the deep-seated popular frustrations bred by a decade of declining living standards, unfulfilled promises, and rampant corruption. Political paralysis, constant calls for the ouster of the president, and a grim outlook for the future became the daily fixtures in a country that only a few months before had been a showcase of the successful transition to a full-fledged market economy. Democracy in Venezuela could no longer be taken for granted.

If such were the consequences of market-oriented reforms in a country well-endowed with natural resources and a democratic tradition, what result can countries such as Egypt, India, Peru, or Russia expect from similar policy changes? Indeed, Venezuela's political instability has been amply cited by critics of market-oriented reforms as evidence of their inappropriateness and their excessive social and political costs. Some have argued that Venezuela's reforms were too drastic and that countries ought to pursue a more gradual approach to avoid economic shocks that result in destabilizing political shocks. The more radical opponents of these policies have insisted that excessive reliance on markets in developing countries is unwarranted, and that the Venezuelan example is a case in point. Defenders of the market-oriented approach blame the political turmoil on the Pérez government. They argue that his government was corrupt and that it failed to pay sufficient attention to the social costs of the changes it implemented. It did nothing to force the benefits of the reforms to trickle down to the poor and the middle class.

These generalizations are misleading and fail to capture the essence of the Venezuelan experience with reforms. Instead, the process and its consequences were dominated by local factors, certain inevitable international trends, and by the structural weaknesses of the state in a developing country. Under these circumstances, Venezuela's apparent advantages proved to be of little use in steering it toward market-led prosperity.

Paper Tigers and Minotaurs

This book uses the Venezuelan experience to explore the complex interaction of politics, economics, and institutions during the initial stages of market-oriented economic reforms. Recent research on the nature of such reforms illuminates the dark conceptual alleys down which policymakers tend to stumble during the design and implementation of such programs. It also identifies which of those alleys are dead ends and exposes certain measures as no more than populist temptations or quick fixes. The costly mistakes that typically accompany such policy indulgences are also well documented.[2] Still lacking, however, is a set of widely accepted propositions about the appropriate politicoeconomic sequencing of the various policy changes, the way in which the economic effects and political consequences of policy changes reinforce or conflict with each other, their implications for institutional design, or the political and institutional preconditions for success. Policymakers seeking analytical guidance to deal with the politics and economics of a drastic policy overhaul will find in the specialized literature a rich repertoire of policies that are optimal from an economic perspective. They can also find a detailed survey of what not to do. But they will not find such elaborate prescriptions on how to incorporate the political and institutional consequences of economic reforms into their decisionmaking.

This dearth of guidance stems both from the relative novelty of these reforms and from their very nature. From the perspective of policymakers, inducing large-scale societal changes through deliberate policy reforms is akin to walking through a constantly shifting maze filled with menacing beasts. When confronted, some of these monsters turn out to be harmless—paper tigers—while others are deadly minotaurs. Whereas paper tigers are often only a distraction, minotaurs force governments to look for ways to avoid the risky and costly confrontations with them or even to exit the policy-reform maze altogether.

The Venezuelan case illustrates how difficult it is to distinguish paper tigers from minotaurs. Observers inside and outside government assumed that the reforms would face stiff opposition. The highly protected and influential private sector was expected to be a formidable enemy of changes that would erode its power and privilege. In practice, however, once these private groups realized that the core changes were largely irreversible, they stopped seeking a return to the old policies. Instead, they concentrated their efforts on seeking delays or revisions of specific policy details and on retaining their hold on specific privileges.

Thus, the dismantling of the highly protectionist regime under which private business had prospered for decades was largely unimpeded. Although this tiger looked and sounded very intimidating, and certain of its actions were threatening, it was unable to stop the government from liberalizing trade. In contrast, no one had suspected that in Venezuela—one of the few Latin American countries that was spared the horrors of the military dictatorships of the 1960s and 1970s—the armed forces would significantly shape the politics of economic reforms. The military minotaur unexpectedly sprang into action twice. Even though it failed to unseat the government and no major policy reversals occurred, it managed to bring further progress to an almost complete halt.

Predicting which measures would be acceptable to the public and which would provoke a hostile outcry was likewise error prone. For instance, no one anticipated that Venezuelans would take to the streets to protest higher gasoline prices and mortgage payments while passively tolerating food and medicine prices that put these staples beyond the reach of many consumers. Popular reaction was so fierce that it forced the government to abandon the plan to increase the price of gasoline (though it would have still been among the world's lowest) and to implement a costly subsidy for home mortgages. Meanwhile, prices of medicine and food continued to increase much faster than the rate of inflation without provoking an even remotely proportional reaction from politicians, the media, or the public.

Corruption was another area in which a huge discrepancy between the anticipated results and the actual consequences of the reforms emerged. Corruption had always existed, and it had flourished at unprecedented levels under the pervasive state controls imposed by previous governments. By doing away with such controls, the Pérez administration eliminated a major source of corruption. Businessmen no longer needed to bribe government officials to import, export, set prices, or obtain loans. The administration assumed this change would inspire support for its reforms. Instead, the negative initial impact of the reforms and their political fallout seemed to cancel out any tolerance Venezuelans may have had for corruption. Pérez and his administration became a political lightning rod for accusations of corruption, which escalated to the point of severely impairing the capacity to govern. Paradoxically, economic policies had never been so immune to the self-interested meddling of bureaucrats and politicians, but never before had the perception of corruption been such an important political factor with such a constraining effect on policymaking.

Foreign banks, multilateral financial institutions, and foreign investors in general were also perceived as minotaurs that could threaten the government's capacity to pursue its own reform agenda. Governments that adopt market-oriented reforms hear frequent criticism that their policy changes are externally imposed and serve the interests of foreign actors first and domestic constituencies second. In Venezuela, these foreign actors were clearly very influential. But, in general, an adversarial relationship with the government failed to materialize given that, in most respects, Pérez's policy approach was consistent with their own preferences.

Nonetheless, this general convergence did not preclude intense conflicts with these international actors. Such conflicts occurred, for example, with foreign commercial banks over debt negotiations, with multilateral financial institutions over loan conditions, and with private foreign firms over the withdrawal of the previous administration's foreign exchange guarantee for imports. Surprisingly, the government prevailed far more often in these conflicts than in its run-ins with seemingly less powerful domestic actors. For instance, the government, the IMF, the World Bank, and others agreed that a value-added tax was critically needed. The president of the lower chamber of Congress did not think so, however. After four years of negotiations, concessions, and exhortations from authoritative domestic and international sources (including the general secretaries of the two main political parties) and with a catastrophic fiscal crisis looming on the horizon, the tax remained in limbo, stymied by his opposition.

As these examples and the pages that follow show, undertaking large-scale policy changes is still an essentially uncharted process filled with risks and counterintuitive surprises. Also, as the cases of South Korea, Chile, and Mexico indicate, structural reforms take a long time to mature, they follow highly unpredictable paths, and they have myriad consequences which, in turn, generate other effects that are impossible to foresee.

The uncertainties inherent in the process of reform and the fact that this study is being published as events in Venezuela are still unfolding qualify the present assessments and conclusions as necessarily preliminary. For example, a few days after the second coup attempt, when the survival of democracy in Venezuela was widely doubted, scheduled elections for state and local officials took place for only the second time in history. Six hundred different local political organizations sponsored several thousand candidates to fill the fifteen hundred positions open for election. Voter turnout was higher than expected and, in general, Venezuelans saw that ballots were more effective than bullets as the means to replace public officials. While Venezuelan democracy is still precarious, the local elections of 1992 played a significant role in anchoring it.

Nineteen ninety-three was the last year of the Pérez presidency, and the future of democracy and of economic reforms in Venezuela will critically depend on the next administration's performance. The political color and the economic policies of the government that succeeds Carlos Andrés Pérez's may be different. But in fundamental respects, the evolution of politics and economics in Venezuela for the foreseeable future will be inextricably linked with the reforms the Pérez administration launched in 1989 and the political changes they set in motion.

The Organization of the Book

Chapter 2 briefly traces the evolution of the modern Venezuelan economy. It gives special attention to the structural characteristics that brought about the accumulated distortions and macroeconomic imbalances that set the stage for the crisis facing the country and the government in 1989. Chapter 3 presents the anatomy of Venezuela's economic crisis and identifies the initial conditions underlying the reforms launched by the Pérez administration. While the Venezuelan crisis had certain peculiarities stemming from the economy's dependence on oil, it was similar in essence to the typical crisis and economic collapse that have beset so many other countries in recent years, forcing them to seek out alternatives to their traditional economic policies. Chapter 4 describes the reform package the government adopted. It also discusses some of the factors that influenced President Pérez's ideological shift and examines the odd composition of the team he assembled to design and manage the reforms. The following chapter offers an overview of the immediate political, economic, and social consequences of the reforms. As the chapter indicates, the economic policies of the new Pérez administration took the whole country by surprise, including some of Pérez's own ministers.

The two failed attempts by groups in the armed forces to overthrow the Pérez government in 1992 were as surprising as Pérez's economic policies. Chapter 6 provides a detailed account of the two failed coups and the unprecedented and equally surprising political and social instability they catalyzed. The army revolts radically altered the prevailing set of opportunities, constraints, and alliances. Chapter

7 analyzes the economic, political, and institutional roots of the attempted coups and discusses the political instability the country experienced during the final years of the Pérez administration, which culminated in his ouster. Chapter 8 concludes the book with a synthesis of the more general lessons that can be derived from this analysis of the Venezuelan reform experience.

Chapter 2
A Reversed-Midas Touch: Venezuela's Recent Economic Evolution

The Venezuelan economy since the 1920s can be summed up in a word: oil. And despite the dramatic policy shift of 1989, intended in part to promote economic diversification, Venezuela will remain dependent on the oil industry for the foreseeable future. For example, taxes from oil sales account for more than 70 percent of total government revenue, and oil exports generate more than 80 percent of the country's total foreign exchange earnings.

Although oil brought Venezuela to the peak of prosperity, it did not cushion the country's plunge into economic crisis. During the 1950s and 1960s, oil exports made the Venezuelan economy one of the most successful in the world, with compounded annual growth averaging a remarkable 6 percent.[3] As the oil industry matured, Venezuela's agriculture-pastoral economy gave way to an extractive-mining economy with a substantial capacity to generate foreign exchange. Most of these earnings accrued to the government, which reinvested or spent them attempting to alleviate poverty, diversify the economy, and buy popular support for itself.

In the late 1970s the boom went bust. Dependence on a single export product had inhibited the creation of policies that might have averted the long-term declines in productivity and economic health that were making themselves felt just as the boom reached its height.

Oil-Subsidized Industrialization

Exploitation of oil began in the 1920s. It rapidly displaced agriculture as the core of the economy and sparked the fastest urbanization process on the continent. The public sector came to rely on oil to finance its activities, removing the government's incentive to develop other revenue sources. This last trend continued through the late 1950s when the new democratic regime adopted an industrialization program of import substitution aimed at building an industrial base that would eventually help diversify the economy.

Venezuela was the last of Latin America's large economies to initiate comprehensive, state-led efforts to industrialize. Nonetheless, they progressed rapidly. The government protected infant industries and provided easy financing terms to private investors. Huge sums of oil revenue were used to finance all manner of government projects, to create a modern infrastructure, to stimulate internal demand, and to pay for necessary imports. As was then typical of many developing countries, state-owned enterprises emerged in almost every economic sector, and the government took over when private firms failed in order to avoid job losses.

The results were impressive. Economic growth was high, and inflation very low, averaging 1.7 percent annually during the 1950s and 1960s. (See figures 1 and 2.) Foreign investment was strong, especially in oil and iron ore. Venezuela's deep dependence on the oil market made its economy extremely vulnerable to international disruptions. Prior to the mid-1970s, however, the world market for oil remained relatively stable. While oil prices were not very high and there were occasional rumblings about deteriorating terms of trade, oil was a substantial, steady source of fiscal solvency and foreign earnings.

Figure 1. Venezuela: Real GDP Growth in Percent, 1970–92
Source: Central Bank of Venezuela.

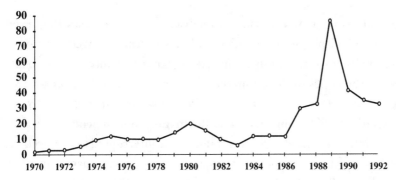

Figure 2. Inflation (CPI Percent Change, 1970–92)
Source: *International Financial Statistics.*

By the mid-1970s, with oil prices rising from $2 a barrel to $14 and higher, the influx of foreign exchange proved almost impossible to manage and invest wisely. An attempt to neutralize the damaging effects of excess oil income on the local economy by investing it outside the country proved unsuccessful. Carlos Andrés Pérez, president from 1974 to 1979, pledged to "administer abundance as if we were administering scarcity." His prudent intention had almost no consequence for the way state institutions or most segments of society actually behaved, however.

Growth remained high during the mid-1970s, at 6.8 percent, largely because of the explosion of oil prices following the first oil price shock; inflation stayed relatively low at 6.6 percent on average. The current account of the balance of payments registered a large surplus, international reserves broke the $9 billion barrier in 1976, and they exceeded $11 billion in 1981 after the second oil crisis. Such an unprecedented accumulation of reserves gave rise to all manner of illusions, false expectations, and consequently, policy mistakes.

Each oil price shock played havoc with expectations and fiscal discipline. Higher oil prices increased government income sharply and unexpectedly, stimulating public expenditures and new capital projects. When oil prices declined, bringing down income, public expenditures and investment outlays failed to subside—in some years they even increased. Expectations, politics, and massive capital investment projects fueled government spending patterns that were incapable of adapting to the cycles of the oil markets.[4] *On average, since 1970 oil revenues have varied from one year to the next by an amount equivalent to 6 percent of GDP*—a wildly unmanageable fluctuation. But the construction of steel mills, dams, and highways could not be interrupted to take account of lower oil prices and their impact on the government's income. Readily available foreign debt was the preferred means of cushioning the macroeconomic jolts caused by this reeling pattern of fiscal income and outlays. By the early 1980s Venezuela owed more than $20 billion to foreign banks. (Even after continuous servicing, several reschedulings, and renegotiations, this debt was still about $30 billion in the mid-1980s).

The steady income from oil allowed the state to continually forestall measures to increase productivity. It also masked the need for changes in the country's economic direction and allowed successive governments to postpone even minor adjustments that might have generated adverse political reactions. This extreme aversion to politically difficult economic decisions led Venezuela to continue an indiscriminate import-substitution policy long after it had ceased to be prudent. Rising tariffs and import quotas, increased state intervention, price controls, massive undirected subsidies, and tax loopholes deepened the economy's underlying structural inefficiencies.

Entire industries lacking any possibility of a self-sustained long-term contribution to the country's economic well-being were encouraged to grow. Ever-increasing subsidies and trade barriers assured their profitability while buffering them from international and even domestic competition. Such schemes had devastating repercussions for productivity.

Between 1975 and 1979, productivity decreased an average of 1.1 percent each year, and from 1983 to 1988 the decline accelerated to 1.4 percent per year. In industrial sectors in which state-owned enterprises dominated, productivity decreased by 9.2 percent annually during the late 1970s and by 1.4 percent annually from 1983 to 1988. From 1979 to 1983 productivity grew at 5.2 percent per year, yielding an average of 0.7 percent for the period 1975 to 1988, a time when South Korea's productivity grew at 9 percent per year, Argentina's at almost 3 percent, and Mexico's at about 2 percent.[5]

Venezuela's experience with import substitution policies was similar to those of most other developing countries, except that it was more extreme. The import substitution scheme did help create an industrial base where none had existed and, in this case, industrial expansion proceeded at an accelerated pace. Between 1960 and 1980, industrial output grew, on average, 7.3 percent each year, increasing the number of jobs in manufacturing by a factor of six between 1950 and 1978.[6] But, in Venezuela, the lingering economic distortions that are usually associated with this policy approach also surfaced with equal speed and intensity. A state that was simultaneously rich in oil and poor in efficient institutions tended to amplify both the virtues and the defects of an industrialization effort that, while initially successful, rapidly became excessively subsidized, grossly inefficient, and ultimately incapable of sustaining growth. The need to consolidate Venezuela's incipient democratic system, for many years a precious oddity among Latin American countries, served to justify policies that, in retrospect, were economically unsound.

Oil-Subsidized Mistakes

Oil wealth made economically dubious policy decisions appear acceptable by blurring their negative consequences. Thus, for many years, the basic challenge of balancing political needs with economic constraints had no place on the agendas of Venezuelan politicians and government officials.[7] The intuitions about economic trade-offs that political leaders tend to develop in cultures where scarcity is more apparent were absent in Venezuela. The demand for sound economic thinking was simply not present. Those individuals—economists and others—who insisted that realities of economics must be respected met with disdain, if not outright contempt.

Not surprisingly, macroeconomic policymaking remained simplistic, primitive, and, in hindsight, extremely slow to adapt to changes at home and abroad. Exchange rates, interest rates, and fiscal, monetary, trade, and industrial policies were rigid and they were poorly (if at all) coordinated. Continuously accumulating imbalances and distortions of all kinds provoked little or no response from the public, politicians, and even most local economists. Industrial policy became a guise for the transfer of public resources to privately owned priority sectors chosen for political reasons. It was only a matter of time before this situation became unsustainable.

For eight continuous years, from 1978 to 1985, the economy shrank. Thus reality started to catch up with Venezuela as GDP declined at a rate of 1 percent a year, while the population grew by more than 2 percent a year. By 1985, real GDP was 25 percent lower than it had been just seven years earlier. Real income per capita in 1985 was almost 15 percent lower than in 1973, when oil revenues had boosted Venezuela to a much higher income level. In a striking example of a reversed-Midas touch, the system had systematically turned gold—or oil—into poverty.

Although problems seemed to emerge everywhere, increasing poverty was the most serious of all. In 1981, the number of people living below the poverty line began to rise steadily, continuing throughout the rest of the decade. By 1989 an estimated 53 percent of all Venezuelans lived in poverty, up from the 32 percent in 1982. And in 1989, 22 percent of all households lacked sufficient income to cover the costs of the minimum daily food requirement, up from 10 percent in 1982. Moreover, throughout the 1980s income distribution grew ever more inequitable, and wealth became even more concentrated than before.[8]

Venezuela's international financial conditions also deteriorated. The effects of capital flight, escalating foreign debt, and the loss of access to international credit markets created another first for modern Venezuelan policymakers: a severe foreign exchange shortage. Capital flight accelerated from 1978 to 1982 when domestic interest rates fell below international levels and the whole incentive structure shifted toward selling the local currency—the bolivar—and buying foreign exchange. The incentives were not only economic. The country also witnessed the baffling scene of the president of the Central Bank exhorting Venezuelans to buy dollars in a move that, according to his understanding of economics, would support the bank's efforts to drain liquidity from the system and curb inflation. The capital flight episodes of the 1980s were repeated and massive. Estimates of the foreign assets privately held by Venezuelans abroad at the end of the decade range from $50 to $80 billion. Foreign debt, which began rising in the early 1970s, increased from about $2 billion in 1973 to over $35 billion in 1982. By the mid-1980s the government was devoting almost 70 percent of all its export revenues to service its foreign debt.

In 1982, Mexico defaulted on its huge foreign debt, precipitating a crisis that had been building for some time. The flow of foreign funds to the entire Latin American region came to an almost complete halt. Unable to borrow abroad, the Venezuelan public sector lost the only instrument with which it had managed its external imbalances and was forced to innovate.

RECADI—An Exchange Rate Fiasco

In 1983, the government of President Luis Herrera Campins, a Christian Democrat, established controls on foreign exchange in an attempt to curb a process that threatened to drain the country of reserves. This exchange rate regime, known as RECADI (*Regimen de Cambios Diferenciales*—multiple rate regime), compounded economic maladies and, not surprisingly, became a magnet for corruption. The system set several different rates for foreign exchange. Importers of priority goods (ranging from medicines to automotive parts) had one exchange rate; importers of goods and services of lesser priority had another. Private firms seeking to service their foreign debt, importers of machinery and capital goods, and the general public had still other exchange rates. Each year the government estimated the amount of foreign exchange available and allotted quotas to each sector (even to individual importers) using criteria that frequently changed and were seldom transparent. Jockeying for the largest quota of foreign exchange at the lowest available rate became the primary objective of the Venezuelan private sector during the 1980s. No other business yielded a higher profit than gaining access to subsidized hard currency. Politicians, union leaders, journalists, radio and television personalities, and beauty queens all used their contacts with and influence over public officials to bias foreign exchange allocations. Opportunities to make a quick fortune were not left unexploited.

Except for exchange controls, the government implemented no other policy changes. It continued to maintain interest rates at levels far below inflation and the valuation of the exchange rate on the free market. The skewed orientation of public spending continued, while mismanaged public enterprises and utilities generated inferior products and large deficits. Foreign debt service imposed growing burdens on the balance of payments and on public finances. As circumstances steadily eroded, new local and foreign private investment grew scarce, social services deteriorated, and, in general, gains in productivity and income distribution came to be found only in politicians' speeches.

During the second half of the 1980s, the government of President Jaime Lusinchi (of the *Acción Democrática* party) further postponed a policy redirection and like its predecessor, offered only partial, isolated reforms. The situation was not untenable enough to prompt politically costly structural reforms. And, in contrast to the early 1980s when the Iran-Iraq War pushed international oil prices to unprecedentedly high levels and helped generate significant government revenues, in the late 1980s oil prices declined sharply. In 1985, Venezuelan oil averaged $33 a barrel; in 1986 the price it fetched dropped to $15. Government revenue from oil declined drastically in 1986, yet public spending increased by 10 percent. (See figures 3, 4, and 5.)

Given that the government had difficulties managing the economy in times of large oil revenues, with greatly diminished oil income confusion reigned. Unfortunately, needed policy reforms were displaced from the government's agenda by prevailing conditions—inertia, ignorance, disagreements over policy alternatives, schemes like price controls and RECADI—all of which made existing aberrations in economic policy very profitable for political, business, media, and labor elites. Moreover, since presidential elections were scheduled for

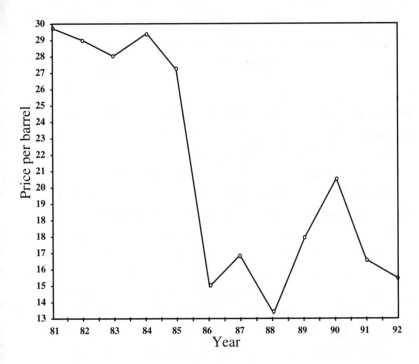

Figure 3. International Oil Prices in U.S. Dollars
Source: *International Financial Statistics.*

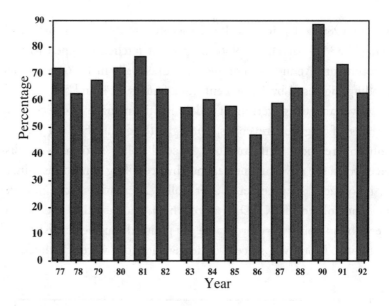

Figure 4. Government Revenue from Oil
Source: *International Financial Statistics.*

December 1988, the public and their leaders knew that no costly, unpopular changes would occur before that date. Quite the opposite, the longstanding practice of tightening government controls while greatly expanding public spending on the eve of elections was set in motion. Despite a sharp decrease in government revenues, major expansions in public spending, credit, and foreign exchange availability occurred, so that in 1988 the economy grew almost 5 percent. Yet Venezuelans seemed astonished when the new government disclosed in early 1989 that foreign currency reserves were severely depleted, that the fiscal deficit for 1988 exceeded 9 percent of GDP, that the current account had registered its largest deficit in history, and that all prices, from interest rates to eggs, from medicine to bus fares, were artificially low and impossible to sustain.

In sum, after decades of consuming more than they produced, to restore balance, Venezuelans' real incomes and consumption would

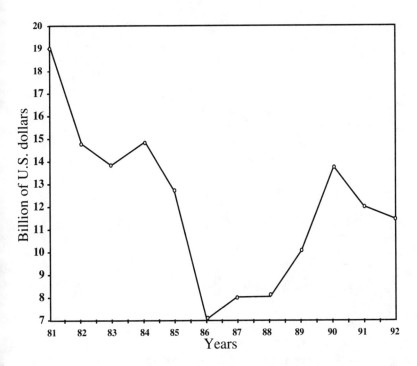

Figure 5. Total Oil Revenue (in current dollars)
Source: *International Financial Statistics.*

have to decline. Few were prepared for the consequences of economic
policies influenced more by harsh realities than by short-term political
considerations.

Chapter 3
Teetering on the Brink of Collapse: 1989

Elections were held on December 3, 1988. Carlos Andrés Pérez won the election with 54.6 percent of the votes, surpassing his main opponent, Eduardo Fernandez, a Christian Democrat, by the largest margin in twenty-five years. Nonetheless, Pérez's political party, *Acción Democrática*, did not fare as well, losing its majorities in both houses of Congress and in many local governments. Pérez's inauguration took place February 2, 1989, before an unprecedented number of world leaders, attesting to the solid international reputation he enjoyed at the time. Popular expectations about the new government were high, and an atmosphere of renewed optimism prevailed. Just three weeks later, on Monday, February 27, the people of Caracas and three other major cities took to the streets in a rampage of riots and looting.

Riots

The three days of civil turmoil left three hundred Venezuelans dead and the country in a state of panic, confusion, and outrage. Such violence was unprecedented. Not even at the height of the turbulence of the 1960s when Castroite guerrillas went to war against the young democratic state had such widespread and violent civil disobedience occurred.

The riots erupted spontaneously; no organization induced people to protest. On February 27, the last Monday of the month, workers living on the outskirts of Caracas were surprised by a substantial increase in bus fares. The government had approved an increase in the fares but the independent bus owner-operators decided to charge more than this. The operators felt that the government increases were not enough to cover their cost increases over several previous months. The twice-raised fares were substantially more than what passengers had been accustomed to paying.

In what later proved to be a systematic flaw of the Pérez administration, the government failed to communicate its decision in a timely and effective manner—the precise details and the reasons for it. Thus, workers only discovered on Monday morning what they had to pay to get to their jobs. The situation was exacerbated by the timing of the increases; being the end of the month, workers were low on cash and most had only the minimum to cover the usual fares and collect their paychecks. Heated arguments broke out between drivers and passengers; these escalated to angry protests and then to physical assaults.

Ineffective police action abetted the escalation. Once violence broke out, it quickly became clear that the police were unable to restore order. Although largely unknown at the time, the Caracas metropolitan police force was in the midst of its most severe institutional crisis ever—the first strike in its history had just ended the week before. Years of budget cuts and managerial ineptitude had left the force with scarce resources, battered morale, and insufficient equipment and trained personnel for a city of five million inhabitants. When the riots began, the issues that had prompted the strike were still unresolved. Furthermore, the DISIP, a national police force that supplies intelligence to the government, was also in crisis and was undergoing a complete overhaul, which immobilized it for several months.

Gangs and roving bands rapidly appeared, taking advantage of the fact that the police were overwhelmed by the street disturbances and were unable to provide surveillance to all sectors of the city. They roamed the city smashing the windows of stores and supermarkets along the streets and in shopping malls. As the day proceeded without any marked police intervention, more and more people got involved; isolated incidents escalated into wholesale looting of supermarkets and even factories near the poor barrios surrounding Caracas.

Live media coverage of the incidents stimulated popular participation in the lootings. Accounts of the events were heard and seen live on radio and television, showing how those involved roved unopposed, prompting others to take to the streets. On the first day (before the army was ordered in) people could see plainly on television that they could simply go to their nearby shopping center, enter the abandoned stores, and take whatever was left.

At no time in recent memory had Venezuela experienced an episode like this. Unexpected and excessive increases in bus fares, the government's failure to communicate its policies, the crisis in the police force, and the catalyzing effect of live media coverage were obvious determinants of the riots. But a more subtle and fundamental factor was the social tension that had been building over an extended period. The conditions contributing to it had reached an unbearable level in the months prior to Pérez's inauguration. During the last part of 1988 and early 1989, Venezuelans experienced the worst shortages of consumer goods they had ever known. Tensions between consumers and merchants had been at a breaking point for months as the anticipation of major price increases, the scarcity of raw materials, and a lax monetary policy stimulated hoarding, put artificial constraints on supply, and increased demand.

The escalation of protests into violence was exacerbated by the government's delay in responding even after the situation was clearly out of control. The president postponed for as long as possible the decisions to call in the army, declare a curfew, and temporarily suspend constitutional guarantees. He knew the army was not trained to deal with civil disobedience and that its intervention would be traumatic. At the same time, he systematically and urgently consulted all the parties in Congress, labor leaders, and private-sector leaders, and many others to gain support for the measures needed to reassert control. This effort took almost a day and a half, during which time no effective government presence was felt in the streets. This contributed to a perception of impunity, further fueling looting and rioting.

The illusions of wealth and economic security had created an artificial and dangerous economic, social, and institutional setting that sooner or later had to collapse. Inflation, capital flight, internal and external deficits, growing poverty, and dilapidated public services were the most visible symptoms of an economy in tatters.

Artificial Prices

Venezuela has had a long history of price controls, an indispensable element of its import substitution strategy. The high tariffs required to protect infant industries reduced and in many cases eliminated outside competition. Over the years, even as infant industries matured, protection and subsidies were allowed to remain. This gave rise to highly concentrated ownership structures, letting a small number of large private firms coordinate their pricing and investment decisions. The lack of price competition, whether foreign or domestic, justified government intervention. The Ministry of Industry officially set prices for an immense, and administratively overwhelming, array of products and services.

While the items under price controls changed over time, the more the government felt that inflation was getting out of control, the longer the list became. The system was by no means immune to periodic price hikes of the controlled products, however. These sudden and sometimes large price increases essentially depended on the producers' bargaining power, itself a function of their political contacts and bribes given to Ministry of Industry officials and others. The most recent version of the price control regime had been established in 1987 and was among the most restrictive ever. There were forty-three broad categories for which producers could not alter prices without ministry approval. Other price increases had to be reported to the ministry, which had the authority to veto them. Not only were such staple goods as bread, milk, and medicines strictly controlled. Also centrally determined were the prices of a cup of coffee at any coffee shop (with a different price if consumed while standing at the counter or sitting at a table), all restaurant items, movie theater tickets, ice, funeral services, toothpaste, batteries, spaghetti, mattress foam, soft drinks, toilet paper, auto parts, beer, laundry services, and so forth.[9] Despite price controls, inflation averaged an unprecedented 23 percent from 1986 to 1988. A 93 percent devaluation of the bolivar in 1986, aimed at restoring equilibrium, added to inflationary pressures.

At the same time, the fact that elections were scheduled for December 1988 had two effects. First, everyone from housewives to foreign exchange speculators perceived that no major policy shifts—price hikes or devaluation—would take place until the first half of 1989. Second, and confirming general expectations, the government's resistance to price increases, begun in late 1987, stiffened throughout 1988, when it essentially attempted a general price freeze. For most of 1988, decisionmakers in government were repeatedly told to adopt what was half-jokingly referred to as "the x-ray exam" stance—don't move, hold your breath, and wait for the election.

Widespread expectations of price increases, artificially low official prices and interest rates, and an expansionary election-year fiscal policy fueled demand. A full set of disincentives and bottlenecks constrained an adequate supply response. The consequences quickly became apparent. Plant shutdowns, hoarding, the breakdown of formal distribution systems, speculation, heightened corruption, and the emergence of black markets for almost all products resulted in the worst shortages Venezuelans had ever experienced. Manufacturers reduced their operations to avoid losses from low prices, merchants held on to inventories awaiting higher prices, and consumers bought all they could before prices increased. As a result, Venezuela, whose poorest citizens had been accustomed to comparatively easy access to staples and consumer goods, experienced for the first time in modern history strict rationing, long lines, and months of anxiety and tension. The widely held suspicion that the products were in stock somewhere awaiting new, higher, prices added to deepening frustration and anger. During the riots, many of the grocery stores in poor neighborhoods were looted in revenge for what was perceived as the speculative behavior of the merchants.

The Collapse of Foreign Exchange Controls

Balance of payments deficits, not a frequent trait of oil exporting countries, occurred every year between 1986 and 1989. Many factors contributed to Venezuela's weakening international finances. Among others were the falling oil prices of the mid-1980s, rising international interest rates, service on a $30 billion foreign debt, reduced access to international credit, severely constrained non-oil exports, and continued lack of investor confidence. The weak balance of payments was also symptomatic of a grossly distorted exchange rate. Many oil exporting countries tend to have overvalued exchange rates, a phenomenon called "Dutch disease" in reference to the overvaluing effects Holland's large gas findings had on the guilder. In Venezuela, this propensity was amplified by RECADI, the exchange-control regime adopted in 1983 and maintained until 1989.

Highly politicized economic decisionmaking and poorly run government organizations weakened the capacity of the state to administer the controls or even to curb the excesses it engendered. Thus, the foreign exchange allocation system became a major source of distortion and economic weakness. Cheap foreign exchange impaired non-oil exports and gave a great incentive to import goods and export capital. In this way, in the midst of an economic crisis and with high import duties still in place, imports soared between 1983 and 1988. Given that most goods were subject to high tariffs and strict quotas, importers sought special permits and waivers from the Ministry of Industry, which dispensed them at its discretion. Imports totalled almost $8 billion in 1986, $9 billion in 1987, and $12 billion in 1988. By comparison, imports to all countries in Latin America in 1988, totalled $115 billion; Venezuela, with only 4 percent of the region's population, accounted for more than 10 percent of the entire region's imports. In contrast, exports other than oil and aluminum remained insignificant.

Persistently high import bills pushed international reserves to critically low levels. At the end of 1988, the current account registered a $6 billion deficit, and the country had lost half of its net international reserves. All along, while the official rate was left virtually unchanged, the "parallel" and relatively free exchange rate was depreciating continuously. At the end of 1988 the differential between the government price of U.S. dollars through RECADI and the free market price was about 110 percent.

A Budget Deficit Beyond Control

In 1985 the fiscal budget enjoyed a surplus equal to 3 percent of GDP; by 1988 this had been replaced by a deficit equal to 9.4 percent of GDP, generating enormous inflationary pressures. The sheer magnitude of the government's current expenditures, growing debt service payments, and the huge losses of public utilities and state-owned enterprises guaranteed ever larger deficits.

Not only had the state's grasp far exceeded its financial and administrative capacities, systematically increasing spending without adequate controls. Government revenues were systematically decreasing while outlays continued to grow. In 1980, the consolidated income of the public sector was 57 percent of GDP. By 1992 it had fallen to 23 percent. The near-exclusive reliance on (the declining) income from oil has played an important part in the fiscal devastation of the Venezuelan state. Public revenues from oil dropped from $1,700 a head in 1981 to $382 in 1992, which also reflects a decline in the price of oil in real terms of 30 percent. (The price of Venezuelan oil went from $30 a barrel in 1981 to about $9 in 1992 measured in 1981 U.S. dollars.) Venezuela's strict adherence to OPEC export quotas and OPEC's successively smaller allocations to Venezuela tended to shrink the country's export volume as well, further eroding income from oil.

A perverse combination of deeply rooted beliefs about the country's state-owned mineral wealth, international isolation, ignorance, and self-interested manipulation by politicians and other public opinionmakers obscured the reality that the state was rapidly moving toward bankruptcy. The majority of Venezuelans, regardless of ideology, income, or educational background, were convinced that no major fiscal problem existed. People believed that the problem, if any, lay on the spending side and not in the size and composition of public revenues. The general conviction was that public spending was too large and wasteful and that any new income accruing to the government would be squandered or stolen by the unholy alliance of politicians, union leaders, and businessmen that controlled state expenditures.

Faced with declining public revenues and incapable of generating new sources of income, successive governments cut spending in areas where the political effects were not immediately visible. This led to schools with teachers, but without blackboards, chalk, or water; universities without laboratories; hospitals without supplies; government offices without telephones or typewriters; and public services without maintenance.

During the 1980s, public revenues were essentially spent in servicing the debt owed foreign banks, paying the public wage bill, investing in the expansion of state-owned enterprises in the Guayana region, and subsidizing the losses of these enterprises as well as those of public utilities, from power plants to garbage collection. Military spending, especially on sophisticated weapons systems, also consumed significant chunks of the budget, even though by international standards it was not high.

Not surprisingly, no serious attempt at tax reform had been made in Venezuela for decades. As a result, in 1992, non-oil public income was a meager 5.6 percent of GDP. In comparison, in Chile, Mexico, or Argentina, tax receipts are approximately 20 percent of GDP, while in such countries as France, Japan, Great Britain, or the United States, they fluctuate between 30 and 40 percent of GDP.

In Venezuela, even the potential income that could have been obtained by lowering the subsidy to the domestic price of gasoline became politically difficult. At the time, gasoline was sold for twenty cents a gallon, which, with the exception of Kuwait, was the lowest price in the world. The government avoided charging domestic consumers prices for fuel and natural gas equivalent to what could be obtained on the export market. This implicit subsidy grew to such an extent that, in 1992, it represented foregoing public revenues amounting to 10 percent of the national budget and 1 percent of GDP. This was as much as the public sector allocated to health that year.[10]

The technical and administrative weaknesses surrounding the process of public budget construction and execution made fighting the fiscal deficit even more difficult. The process was governed by an irrational array of laws, regulations, institutions, and protocols whose impact was to neutralize any attempt at rationalizing government spending and investment. Furthermore, since the Ministry of Public Finance had for more than a decade concentrated almost exclusively on the negotiation of the foreign debt and the administration of the foreign exchange regime, its capacity actually to manage the country's public finances was practically nonexistent. The tax collection department was a shambles; the customs administration was rotten to its core. Staffing was managed from the offices of the political party in power, and in general, corruption and incompetence reigned.

Financial Repression

Previous governments had maintained interest rates at artificially low levels and instituted quotas to direct credit to specific priority sectors at even lower rates. Interest rates were set well below inflation, so domestic borrowing to buy foreign exchange was a no-loss proposition. The depletion of international reserves did not take long; capital flight was further stimulated by interest rates that were low both in comparison to expected inflation and international interest rates. Real interest rates measured -15 percent in 1987 and -12.5 percent in 1988. The poor and the middle class bore the burden of these misguided policies whose stated intentions were to protect them: while their savings might earn 13 percent annually, inflation was twice that rate; credit at the official, low interest rate was for all practical purposes impossible to obtain. Credit was chiefly available to persons with links to the shareholders and managers of private banks, or with foreign exchange to guarantee their loans, or with the political connections to gain entry to state-owned banks. Private banks instituted commissions and processing fees that allowed them, in effect, to charge a higher interest rate than the official one. They were thus able to fund themselves at the low official rate and lend at significantly higher ones—not a bad deal for a select few.

Banks and financial institutions were largely unsupervised and tended to develop highly distorted and unhealthy financial and organizational structures. Government controls on interest rates prevented price competition among banks, while their access to relatively cheap private savings let them invest profitably in a variety of ways, mostly outside the banking industry. This created great incentives for banks to spend heavily on advertising, news agencies, and advanced information systems that would help attract deposits.

Meanwhile, the lack of governmental supervision and an inadequate regulatory framework allowed the financial sector to become severely undercapitalized. In 1982 the total capital base of the Venezuelan financial system was about $1.8 billion. By 1992, it had decreased by 30 percent to $1.2 billion, while in just three years, from 1988 to 1992, total deposits had increased from $6 billion $16 billion. Regulatory failures also permitted financial institutions to accumulate immense portfolios of bad loans. Furthermore, loan portfolios had heavy concentrations of stock in companies related to the institutions' shareholders and their associates. It was not unusual for a failed business initiative owned by individuals or groups with influence in the creditor bank to have its loan paid off with whatever assets were left from the venture if the value of the assets was much less than the debt. These trends generated a continuous erosion of banks' return on investments, while providing huge unrecorded profits for majority shareholders, their friends, and other company insiders.

By misregulating the financial system, the state had constrained its growth, distorted its natural expansion, inhibited its competitiveness, and created conditions that made it vulnerable to massive losses. It became too easy for individuals in the private sector, in concert with their public-sector accomplices, to bias the functioning of the financial system against the poor and the middle class.

Stunted Industrial Development

No economic or social progress could be hoped for unless the intricate web of controls and regulations that stifled the emergence of an internationally competitive private sector could be dismantled. Profound structural changes were urgently needed to alleviate problems caused by the highly concentrated, oligopolistic industrial structure, low overall productivity, and significant obstacles to non-oil exports that had been cultivated over many years of government mismanagement.

With respect to trade, a regime of tariff and nontariff barriers (including mandatory licenses for most imports and duties as high as 940 percent) insulated Venezuela's industry against more efficient international competition. The protectionist regime stunted the growth of the non-oil export sector. Tariffs increased the costs of imported raw materials and put local exporters at a cost disadvantage vis-à-vis their international competitors. Exporters also had to reckon with ports that were both costly to use and unreliable; an inefficient state-owned shipping company; and power, water, and telecommunications services that, while cheap, were also plagued by breakdowns and outages. In many sectors, companies were obliged to purchase inputs from state-owned monopolies (iron, steel, aluminum, chemicals, and petrochemicals) which often failed to meet adequate quality standards and required elaborate bureaucratic red tape.

Such conditions affected not only exporters but the economy as a whole. Together with macroeconomic problems, these structural defects accounted for Venezuela's declining productivity over a period of many years. They also help explain why the country had the same number of industrial establishments in 1989 as a decade before (around ten thousand) and why it went from being one of the region's most attractive sites for foreign investment until the mid-1970s, to one of the least by the late 1980s, numbering among those countries with the lowest influx of direct investment in South America. (The only country in the rather sluggish Andean region of the 1980s to attract less foreign investment than Venezuela was Bolivia.)

Rampant Poverty

Economic mismanagement was also at the root of plunging incomes. During the 1980s, the "lost decade," income per capita throughout Latin America dropped an average of 9.4 percent; in Venezuela it dropped by 20 percent. The clearest indicator of the tremendous threats facing the country, and the most ominous sign for its future, was the continued rise in poverty. By 1988, the number of households living below the poverty line had increased tenfold since 1981; real per capita income had sunk to 1973 levels; and the infant mortality rate was twice that of Jamaica or Costa Rica, countries whose per capita incomes were half that of Venezuela's.

The performance of the Venezuelan state in alleviating poverty during the 1980s is appalling, especially in comparison to countries with lower levels of GNP per capita. It is all the more so considering the state's relatively high volume of public spending in the category of social expenditures for many decades. For more than thirty years, Venezuela spent 10 to 14 percent of its total GDP on so-called social programs. For instance, as data from the World Bank shows, in the health sector, Venezuela spent *three times* more per capita in 1985 than Chile, Jamaica, or Panama. But in 1988, Venezuela's infant mortality was 200 percent higher than Jamaica's, 80 percent higher than Chile's, and 30 percent higher than Panama's.

The mismanagement of public expenditures is even more evident in the area of education: between 1980 and 1986, Venezuela was the only Latin American country to increase significantly its share of total public expenditures on education. In addition, no country in the region spent more per student than Venezuela; its $230 average in 1985, was considerably more than Costa Rica ($100), Chile, Argentina, and Jamaica ($50). Unfortunately, as in the health sector, the performance of public education institutions gave little evidence of these high levels of spending. Illiteracy rates, school enrollment percentages, and other qualitative and quantitative indicators of the effectiveness of primary and secondary schools (such as repetition and dropout rates) were among the worst in the region.

Moreover, even if the experience in many countries shows that the social rate of return is much higher in primary schools than in universities, Venezuela still allocated the largest share of GDP to higher education (an average of 2.5 to 3 percent) in the Latin American region. All other countries except Costa Rica (with 1.9 percent) devoted less than 1 percent in the 1980s. In 1987, the government spent ten times more on each student enrolled in higher education institutions than what it spent on children attending elementary schools (Bs. 31,000 versus Bs. 3,100). This skewed proportion is a reflection of the political impact of university students visibly and vocally protesting budget cuts, their professors' ability to write persuasive editorials in local newspapers defending their budgets, and a weak or irresponsible state.

The Venezuelan poverty rates reflect this generalized social tragedy: the proportion of extreme and critical poverty increased from 32.6 percent in 1982 to 53.7 percent in 1989. Those in urban areas were the most affected: compared with 1979, the population living in urban slums increased by 44 percent in 1984, representing 56 percent of the total urban population. By the late 1980s, eight out of every ten poor families lived in urban areas.

In sum, at the start of 1989, Venezuela was in obvious economic danger, operating with an increasingly isolated and grossly inefficient economy on the brink of hyperinflation and socioeconomic collapse. The partial, half-hearted reforms of past administrations would no longer suffice. Under these conditions the Pérez government unveiled *El Gran Viraje*, "The Great Turnaround."

Chapter 4
El Gran Viraje:
The Great Turnaround

The Pérez government called its reform program, *El Gran Viraje*, "The Great Turnaround." Popularly, the reforms were known as *el paquete*, "the package," an expression used colloquially to refer to a problematic, cumbersome situation. Both names proved appropriate. Few observers anticipated that The Turnaround would be so abrupt or that the package would be so problematic. The new policy orientation was a radical and sweeping departure from the past which created confusing and harsh conditions. Nothing in recent memory prepared Venezuelans for it.

While Pérez had insisted during the 1988 electoral campaign that profound changes were needed to modernize the economy, and that if elected he was going to implement them, he had been careful not to go into too much detail. Given the orientation of his previous presidency, his party's attitudes, and the success with which local elites historically had fought attempts at curbing their privileges, Pérez's statements were construed as electoral rhetoric, not as the deep personal commitment they turned out to be.

Pérez's Ideological Shift

In his second presidency, Pérez's actions proved his determination to take whatever measures were needed to deal with the deeply rooted causes of the nation's long-term economic and social deterioration. But more than a belief in the workings of the market per se, profound disillusion with the capacities of the state in a developing country seemed to guide his economic thinking and policy actions.

In the ten years following his first presidency (1974-79), Pérez became intensely involved in international political activities, especially through his role in the international organization of Social Democratic parties. These activities put him in contact with a diverse group of world leaders, and he was able to witness at close hand the profound changes in realities and ideologies occurring worldwide. This exposure set the stage for Pérez's reconsideration of his own beliefs about the role of markets and states.

No single individual guided Pérez's new thinking. Undoubtedly influencing his new vision, however, were the governing experiences of two of his closest personal and political friends: the catastrophic failure of President Alan Garcia in Peru and the successful reforms of Felipe Gonzalez in Spain. Pérez was able to follow the policies and performance of these two governments very closely, and his privileged vantage point allowed him to judge the consequences of the two radically different approaches. Once elected, Pérez displayed an unusual willingness to incur the political costs that inevitably accompany major reforms. He clearly believed that these short-term political costs would be more than compensated for in the future. He sought historical recognition as the leader responsible for wresting the country from the path of decline down which it had fallen—for which the policies of his first administration were partly to blame.

Pérez was always explicit about the personal goal that guided his actions. When asked for his reaction to the attorney general's request for a criminal trial against him in March 1993, during the last few months of his term, his response was strong, and typical.

> I have said many times I am a man with only one ambition—history. I want to go down in history as a man who was capable of overcoming the worst crisis in Venezuela's contemporary history. I want to go down in history as the man who left a legacy and adopted the appropriate actions for Venezuela's modernization and decentralization process. I want history to state that the irreversible changes currently taking place in our country were the result of the courage—with due modesty—with which I handled this phase of our national life. . . . During my administration, the country was decentralized, the

presidency's omnipotent power was broken, the state discretionary power was eliminated, provincial posts and state governorships were opened to popular elections, and mayors of cities, towns, and municipalities were chosen through direct elections. I am the president who has had to face and overcome the greatest number of crises during a [presidential term].[11]

Unfortunately, the evolution of Pérez's thinking about economic policy found little support in the beliefs and attitudes of Venezuela's political, economic, labor, or even, academic elites. In fact, Pérez's own party, *Acción Democrática*, having spent most of the 1980s profiting from the many opportunities to serve as broker between society and the state, adamantly opposed any changes resulting in reduced government intervention.

Moreover, Pérez failed to adapt his political tactics and operating style to the economic realities the country now faced. The assumptions underlying his administration's economic strategy were in tune with the times. But in hindsight, it is clear that the assumptions on which its political strategy was based were poorly attuned to people's expectations and the capacity of the country's institutions for change. This proved to be a fatal inconsistency.

Pérez's Cabinet

The first sign that Pérez was willing to go beyond vague electoral promises came with the appointment of his key ministers. In a surprise to political observers, and even some of the appointees themselves, the new president selected a group of relatively young, foreign trained, politically inexperienced professionals with no party affiliations. Most were academics or respected professional managers in the private sector; for many of them, the appointment was their first public-sector job. This was an abrupt departure from the established practice of placing political activists in the main government posts.

Appointing a cabinet composed of independent technocrats recruited from think tanks, universities, and professional organizations (and not from the ruling party) has become a standard feature in most Latin American and Eastern European countries that have introduced major policy reforms. These technocrats add to the technical capacity of the state, and in some cases they may increase its relative autonomy, enabling the government to adopt policies that longtime bureaucrats captured by vested interests would tend to block. Nonetheless, the technocrats often lack the political skills, the bureaucratic experience, or the capacity to communicate effectively with the general public, creating other problems for the reform process.

Pérez also included in his cabinet individuals who adamantly opposed his reforms. While some of them were longstanding members of *Acción Democrática*, their appointments were more the result of the president's own calculations and needs rather than the specific requests of the party's hierarchy.

Cabinets and government teams are seldom cohesive and well integrated. Instead, political considerations, personal factors, and the other criteria that go into forming a government team tend to create a fragmented and heterogeneous group. Ministers often meet some of their colleagues for on the first time the day they are inaugurated. The fragile solidarity among cabinet members soon becomes a casualty of the turf battles among bureaucracies and the personal rivalries that plague the workings of governments everywhere. The devastating effects that such divisiveness has on performance tend to be contained through a variety of coordinating mechanisms and other formal and informal systems to mediate or contain conflicts within an administration. But no administrative device can compensate for the effects of cabinet members with diametrically opposite views of the methods and instruments that should be used to attain the government's objectives.

Not only did Pérez adopt an economic reform program that the population did not expect and did not like and to which his own party was opposed, he also gave prominent roles to individuals well known for their associations with the policies that his administration was trying to dismantle. While Pérez allowed them to pursue policies that were inconsistent with the overall direction of the government's program he kept these to a minimum and systematically overturned the attempts of some of his ministers to derail the reforms. Nonetheless, certain ministers proved very effective in slowing the process, distorting some aspects of its implementation, and in contributing to the adverse political climate that surrounded it. In fact, after Congress, the cabinet was the most important source of distortions and delays in the execution of the reforms.

The Anatomy of a Policy Shock

While the set of policies adopted by the Pérez government implied a radical break with the immediate past, they had similar goals, assumptions, and design as other reform programs adopted in the late 1980s and early 1990s in Latin America or, for that matter, throughout the world. There were, of course, special traits of the Venezuelan program, but its basic design resembled the Washington consensus developed and promoted by the International Monetary Fund, the World Bank, and certain academic institutions and think tanks.[12]

Macroeconomic stabilization, fiscal balance, trade liberalization, deregulation, privatization, and a social policy targeted at the most vulnerable populations were the building blocks. The intention was to move from a state-led, inward-oriented strategy to one led by export growth. The state would concentrate on those functions that the private sector could not adequately perform.

Accordingly, the initial phase of the Venezuelan program was aimed at restoring macroeconomic stability and eliminating price distortions. The set of measures included establishing a single floating exchange rate, removing price controls on all private goods and services except for eighteen staple items (later reduced to five), letting the market determine interest rates, reducing real public spending, and increasing the prices of public-sector goods to levels that would recover their direct production costs. The complete overhaul of the tax system, including the adoption of a value-added tax, would ensure that government revenues would cease to depend inordinately on oil industry tax revenues and hopefully help alleviate the state's fiscal crisis. Fiscal and monetary expansion were to be administered prudently, and the foreign debt burden was to be reduced through negotiation, which would also restore normal relations with foreign creditors and the international financial community.

Macroeconomic stabilization measures were to be complemented by major structural reforms: trade liberalization; deregulation of the capital, goods, and labor markets; reform of the agricultural, industrial, and financial sectors; foreign investment promotion; and an ambitious privatization program. The general and inefficient price subsidies traditionally used to aid the poor were to be abandoned in favor of efforts focused directly on the most vulnerable groups of society. Social safety nets designed to provide financial, food, and medical assistance to those severely affected by the hardships of reform would also be put in place. Furthermore, Pérez announced governmental and political reforms, public-sector restructuring, and general institutional modernization as part of his government's goals.

A Macroeconomic About-Face

Changes of this magnitude were incredible, and few believed Pérez's resolve was real. The government acted with dizzying speed. It eliminated exchange controls and established the free convertibility of the bolivar, freed interest rates, liberalized virtually all prices, and increased rates for electricity, water, telephone, gasoline, public transportation, and most other public services. Immediately thereafter, the bolivar underwent a 170 percent devaluation, and interest rates climbed from 13 percent to more than 40 percent.[13]

The administration eliminated nontariff barriers on 94 percent of manufactured imports, did away with special permits for exports, and simultaneously restructured the tariff system, lowering average tariffs from more than 35 percent in 1988 to less than 12 percent in 1992. It scheduled (and followed through on) yearly tariff reduction rounds, which along with Venezuela's entry into the GATT, generated the freest trade regime in its recent history. (See figure 6.) The authorities also secured assistance from the International Monetary Fund, the World Bank, and the Inter-American Development Bank.

At the same time, the government began intensive negotiations with foreign commercial banks to reduce and restructure its $19.5 billion public debt. These eventually produced an agreement that changed the composition of the debt, lowered annual interest payments, and secured a seven-year grace period on payments of the principal.[14] Figure 7 shows the reduction in external debt service as a function of total exports from 1988 to 1991.

By early 1990, a new foreign investment regime was in place which had eliminated almost all restrictions on foreign investors and

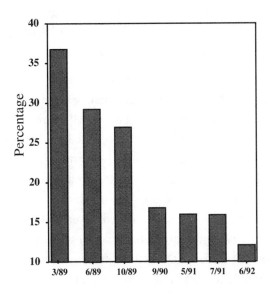

Figure 6. Trade Liberalization (Average Tariffs, 1989–92)
Source: World Bank.

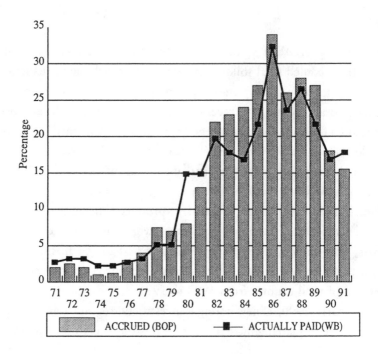

Figure 7. Interest Payments as a Percent of Exports
Source: Inter-American Development Bank.

minimized government interference in financial, commercial, and technological transactions. No government screening or approval of foreign investment projects was required; all restrictions on profit remittances and capital repatriation were lifted; and the stock market was opened to foreign investors for the first time.

New legislation put before Congress proposed a completely different income tax system and the introduction of a value-added tax. Concrete steps to privatize state-owned enterprises initially yielded fast results. By 1991 four commercial banks, the national airline, the ports, the phone company, the cellular telephone system, a shipyard, and several sugar mills and hotels had been privatized. In late 1991, the Pérez administration announced a privatization schedule applying to sugar mills, hotels, several horse racing tracks, another airline, the Caracas water supply system, the regional power companies, the public television network, and many other enterprises and utilities. If everything went according to plan, one or more privatizations *per month* could take place. It seemed incredible that only a short time before, one former president had explained that the phone company could never be sold for national security reasons, that another had equated a proposal to privatize the airline with selling the Venezuelan flag (while neglecting to mention that it was giving away nine thousand tickets a year to politicians, journalists, and their families), and that a third former president had declared that no utility would ever interest a private buyer.

Unfortunately, after this successful start, the ambitious privatization program of the government was derailed, one of the main casualties of the political instability that shook the country during 1992. Even though the government insisted on continuing it, circumstances worked against further progress. Pérez was forced to replace the minister who had successfully led the program, Congress effectively blocked some of the privatization initiatives, and investor interest dropped off as institutional uncertainty and political risk mounted. Nonetheless, the speed, effectiveness, and positive results of the initial wave of privatizations were an unexpected success and a strong precedent for the long term.

On the social front, the government drastically altered policies that had been in place for decades. In the past, governments protected the poor by controlling prices while subsidizing producers. Artificially low prices were also maintained for all public services. Access to housing and other social programs was brokered by the political party in power. These schemes doubled poverty in Venezuela in the 1980s, despite massive public spending, and they also left the majority of the poor woefully vulnerable to the initial consequences of the new policies aimed at correcting such distortions.

The Pérez administration eliminated indirect subsidies to firms producing staple goods (corn flour, milk, sugar, poultry, sardines) and liberalized prices. To cushion the impact of this double shock it instituted a massive nutritional grant program providing cash transfers to mothers of young children in poor urban and rural areas. It also began a program of free medical and nutritional aid to pregnant and nursing women and to small children. In 1991, the coverage of the direct subsidy programs for food reached 69 percent of the target population or 2.5 million of a total of 3.6 million primary school students. Similarly, the ratio of social-sector spending in global public expenditures increased from 11 percent in 1989 to 16 percent in 1990 and 22 percent in 1992. Unemployment compensation payments and other measures to assist laid-off workers were also initiated.

The government set about reforming itself as well, submitting a new law to Congress to amend the existing division of responsibilities within the central government. Some ministries implemented reforms in their structures and standard operating procedures. President Pérez was the catalyst in the process of change that led in December 1989 to the first direct elections of state governors (previously presidential appointees) and other state and local officials, including mayors. National debate commenced over a reform in the electoral law that would provide for the election of members of Congress by name instead of by party-determined list. Eventually, the reform was passed, albeit with provisions that allowed political parties to appoint some members of Congress. Nevertheless, these political reforms were not sufficient to compensate for the extremely negative perceptions Venezuelans had of the government, its reforms, and politicians in general.

The Shock Approach: By Choice or By Default?

The shock approach to economic reforms in Venezuela was driven more by the lack of the administrative capacity to introduce reforms gradually than by an ideological commitment to economic shock therapies. While the debate over gradualism versus the shock treatment in policy reform was raging in the media and professional circles in Venezuela and abroad, it presented no major dilemma to the government. Implementing a more gradual approach to the correction of macroeconomic distortions required a state apparatus with the ability to fine-tune macroeconomic policies and the administrative capacity to manage incremental change. In Venezuela, such institutional and organizational prerequisites had succumbed in the abuse of more than a decade of excesses.

For example, even though the elimination of price controls was an element of the program from the beginning, the decision to do away with them in one fell swoop was not based on a doctrinaire belief in shock therapy. It was forced by the collapse of the administrative system on which these controls relied.

The system had relied on a nationwide network of several thousand public officers charged with the enforcement of the prices set by the Ministry of Industry. These officers periodically inspected all sorts of companies and stores, from funeral parlors to movie theaters, from open-air markets to five-star hotels. Over the years, the government lost control of this operation. Recruitment, promotion, and general management of the price-enforcing agency, the Superintendency of Consumer Protection, became one of the spoils that accrued to the party that held the presidency. Party bosses in the different states hand-picked party members for appointment as price inspectors. Even though the salary was low, these price inspectors all had lavish lifestyles well beyond the means provided by their meager official pay. Such an appointment was one of the most sought-after rewards for services to the party, the profit potential of which was surpassed only by the posts of those few administrators at the Ministry of Industry in charge of deciding what the official price would be for a bottle of ketchup, a block of ice, a battery, or any of the thousands of other items that had to be priced—and revised—periodically.

This system performed important political functions and was maintained for many years. It gave the government great control over the private sector and it provided political parties with effective mechanisms to reward members and gain support. Its original economic purpose, however, became increasingly difficult to attain as inflation was fueled by macroeconomic forces that no administrative system could ever hope to contain.

Once repressed inflation reached very high levels, hoarding and black market speculation became rampant, rationing and empty shelves in stores were common, and the specter of food riots ceased to be a hypothetical possibility. There was little a national corps of price inspectors—even an honest and competent one—could have done. Additionally, the procedure through which prices were set by the Ministry of Industry was largely a technical and administrative fiction. Prices tended to be a function of the moods and interests of ministry officials or the result of instructions coming down from government or the party. No rational set of guidelines and procedures actually existed, and any pretense of a technically based methodology had been abandoned long since. Under these circumstances, maintaining price controls on a large set of items was administratively impossible.

Similar conditions held with respect to the controls on foreign exchange, interest rates, and the financial sector in general. The systems were based on bygone realities; utilizing them under these new circumstances was not feasible. Even if the government had been willing to tolerate the economic, political, and social distortions the controls caused, it lacked the organizational capabilities to administer them.

The interdependence of economic elements also precluded incremental adjustment. Once one area of economic policy is drastically altered, it becomes even more difficult to reform policies in other areas at a slower pace. Once the decisions were made to float the exchange rate and to allow the free convertibility of the currency, the need for real positive interest rates—that is, higher than the inflation rate—became imperative. Moreover, the task of defining the official, controlled prices for goods and services had become overwhelming with fixed exchange and interest rates; a floating currency and changing interest rates would complicate it immensely. Finally, if prices were to be freed, imports also had to be liberalized in order to inject competitive pressures into local markets.

This train of thought, the absence of effective public institutions, the collapse of existing controls, and a government that perceived these realities and accepted the political consequences of taking corrective actions help explain how the rapid transition from one macroeconomic policy set to another—which in this case contributed to rapid stabilization—was achieved. In contrast, the slower pace of efforts to secure fiscal balance and the legal framework that regulated labor relations contributed to the social and political instability that afflicted the country. Fiscal imbalances fueled inflation and inadequate labor laws made the rehabilitation of public agencies—especially those in charge of assisting the poor—almost impossible. Together they played havoc with the government's efforts at building a safety net for the poor.

Chapter 5
The Consequences of Turning the Economy Around

The year 1989 not only brought profound changes in economic policies and living conditions, it was also a year in which unprecedented political transformation took place. It is not easy for a society to digest so much fundamental change all at once. Changes in daily life engender such uncertainty that understanding and expectations cannot keep pace with the new realities, breeding confusion and frustration. Societal change on such a scale is almost by definition disjointed, traumatic, and extremely difficult to manage well, if it can be managed at all.

In a single month—March 1989—Venezuelans saw prices rise 21 percent, as great an increase as they had been accustomed to seeing within an entire year. Although the pace of inflation slowed in following months, the rate for 1989 as a whole was more than 80 percent, the highest ever. Prices were springing back from two years of artificial repression, and they reflected as well the major cost increases of utilities, raw materials, intermediate products, and all services—from insurance policies to transportation costs—as well as higher interest rates and a devalued currency. The 1989 budget was 10 percent smaller in real terms than 1988's; together with the added oil revenues in local currency produced by the devaluation, this helped lower the public-sector deficit from its 1988 level of 9.3 percent of GDP to 1.3 percent.

The economy shrank by almost 10 percent as GDP fell by 8.6 percent in real terms and non-oil GDP contracted by 9.8 percent. These changes impoverished much of the country. The figures for unemployment show only a negligible increase, 9.6 to about 10 percent between 1988 and 1989. But they conceal the fact that thousands of workers lost higher paying jobs and were forced to accept new jobs and pay cuts of as much as one-half (see figure 8). Personal disposable income, which had contracted by about 2 percent the year before, shrank by an overwhelming 14 percent in 1989.[15] Real salaries declined by 11 percent in 1989, bringing their decade-long total decline to 45 percent.[16] More importantly, the real income of urban workers—who constitute 90 percent of the work force—fell below its 1980 level. This may have been the most severe adjustment in labor incomes of any country in Latin America.[17] The government's explanations that the economic and social costs of not undertaking the reforms would have been much higher than the actual consequences of the program may have seemed plausible to some informed international analysts. It was not a very convincing argument for the majority of Venezuelans, however.

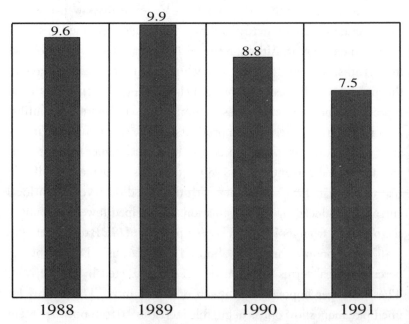

Figure 8. Unemployment, 1988–91 (Percentage of labor force)
Source: CORDIPLAN.

Public Outcry and Crime Waves

Social and political upheaval ensued. The country witnessed strikes and demonstrations by groups of teachers, hospital workers, professors, students, farmers, pharmacists, police officers, homeowners, public-sector employees, and many others. They blamed the government for the real or perceived threats that the new policies posed for their living standards.

Interestingly enough, however, though tensions mounted and protests erupted throughout 1990 and 1991, no major riots or violent clashes between police and marchers materialized. The massive early outburst of violence had apparently so shocked all segments of society that many political leaders avoided actions that might lead to a renewed outbreak. The February 1989 riots had been traumatic because of the uncontained mayhem, loss of life, and property damage. On a more mundane level, most grocery stores and supermarkets were pillaged and had to be closed, making it very difficult to obtain essential items for months afterward, especially for the poor. Small stores located in poorer sections had great difficulty reopening and many never did. The fact that relatively minor incidents triggered the escalation to spontaneous rioting seemed to have imbued organizers of strikes and public marches with a sobering dose of caution and self-restraint.

In fact, one noteworthy feature of this initial phase of reform was the relative absence of organized, violent opposition, especially considering that the government was imposing sweeping changes on a society that was far from convinced of the need for them. This initial phase of nonviolent dissent stands in stark contrast to the two attempted coups of 1992 and the constant public demonstrations that characterized the last years of the Pérez government.

In a related development, personal crime increased dramatically, creating yet another source of dissatisfaction with the government and its policies. The number of street crimes, muggings, and break-ins surged—an unexamined, but important, sociopolitical effect of reforms. The manifest incompetence of the police and the ineffectiveness of the judicial system created an atmosphere of impunity and lawlessness. Inflation, unemployment, the breakdown of social services, and poverty pushed many to seek sustenance through crime. The virtual absence of preventive measures and punishment blurred the disincentives to commit criminal offenses against people and property. Thus, Venezuela's principal cities slipped toward the norm for Latin America as they became places where personal safety was a luxury only few could afford. Together with the increase in the disturbances in public order, the rise in crime rates created a pervasive feeling of chaos and anarchy that fueled both the dissatisfaction with the government and the sense that it lacked the sensitivity or the power to provide for the safety of the population. In many surveys, Venezuelans rated concerns for personal safety above inflation as the country's most important problem.

Early Macroeconomic Successes

On the macroeconomic front, positive results of The Turnaround were soon evident. After the 8.3 percent drop in output in 1989, economic growth leaped forward. GDP grew 6.5 percent in 1990 and 10.4 percent in 1991, the highest rate the Venezuelan economy had ever experienced and one of the highest rates in the world. In 1992, seemingly impervious to the most severe political instability to beset it in decades, the economy continued to grow, this time by 7.3 percent. (Figure 9 shows GDP growth from 1981 to 1992. Table 1 gives average inflation and growth after the early 1980s oil boom.)

While the country's external position as reflected in its balance of payment problems in 1988 was severely damaged, its capacity to generate significant amounts of foreign exchange was never impaired. Together with the reforms, this proven export capacity generated a level of creditworthiness that allowed for a speedy debt renegotiation and the rapid restoration of the country's image in international financial circles. Furthermore, in Venezuela, a devaluation has a net positive

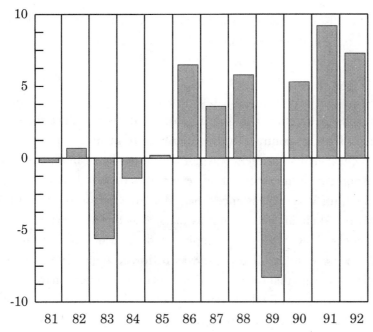

Figure 9. Growth of GDP (Percentage)
Source: CORDIPLAN.

Table 1. The Post-Oil Boom Period (1983–91)

		Average Yearly Inflation	Average Yearly Rate of Growth
1983–1985	Adjustment Without Structural Change	10.0	− 2.3
1986–1988	Deficit-Financed Growth	23.0	5.3
1989–1991	Adjustment and Structural Change	53.1	2.1

Source: CORDIPLAN.

effect on fiscal accounts, since the foreign exchange the state oil company brings in generates more government revenues measured in local currency; these tend to be higher than the government outlays in foreign exchange. Thus, the lifting of the exchange controls and the concomitant devaluation not only corrected the gross distortion of the exchange rate but also gave a boost to efforts to reduce the fiscal deficit. Thus, in contrast to the experience of many other countries, the Venezuelan adjustment was not overly burdened by the external environment.[18] Quite the contrary, external factors—oil prices boosted by the Gulf War, for instance—played a large part in the growth of 1991. But their impact was not as massive as during previous world oil shocks. Nevertheless, in keeping with a recurrent pattern, the sudden increase in oil income was followed by an even steeper decline—a trend that successive Venezuelan governments have always failed to recognize. Public budgets had grown by more than the windfall, and commitments had been made (mostly to expand PDVSA, the state oil company) that could not easily be undone after the short-lived boom in revenues ended.

This time, the role of other sources of growth besides oil, the policy framework, and general expectations contributed to a somewhat different pattern of growth than in past episodes of this kind. Interestingly enough, in 1992 oil-GDP contracted and, for the first time in many years, growth was sustained by the non-oil components of the economy, notably industry and services, especially telecommunications. Indeed, the policies adopted in 1989—if maintained—could generate other sources of economic growth over the long run. Nonpetroleum exports, for example, increased 49 percent in 1989 and 15 percent in 1990. In the following years, however, a sharp decline in the international price of aluminum, a product which accounts for a substantial share of non-oil exports, led to their decline. (Figures 10 and 11 show total exports and the changing shares of non-oil exports.)

Moreover, private-sector exports showed signs of great vitality and potential, growing by 78 percent and 26 percent in 1989 and

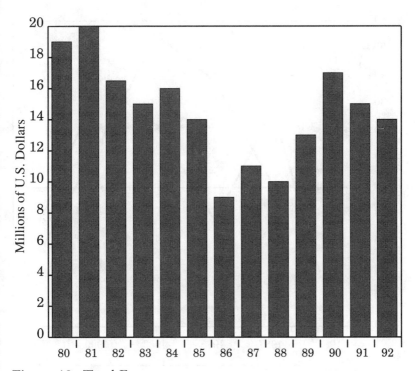

Figure 10. Total Exports
Source: World Bank.

1990, respectively, the first two years in which the reforms applied. (See figure 12.) To some extent, however, this extremely high rate of growth was artificially induced. The abnormal increase in non-oil exports in 1989 and 1990 was propelled by three nonrecurrent factors. First, the combination of a strong domestic recession, the high levels of inventory that firms had stockpiled in anticipation of a devaluation, and the increases in the interest rate made it extremely costly to carry such inventories, exerting strong pressure to market them abroad. Second, a substantial fiscal incentive to exporters was in place which, along with the devaluation, generated very high profit margins in exports. Third, the existing system encouraged the overinvoicing of

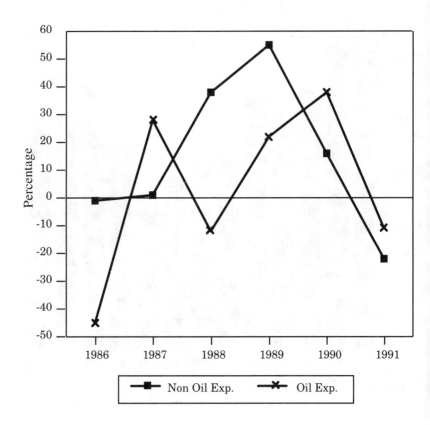

Figure 11. Export Growth Rates
Source: World Bank.

exports, amplifying and distorting the relevant statistical data. After 1989 the domestic economy entered a high-growth phase and excess inventories and output that had been exported were redirected to the domestic market. The policy framework to stimulate exports was totally modified, eliminating marginal exporters as well as the tendency to overinvoice. The very rapid growth of private-sector exports was not sustainable beyond the initial years. The expansion of the domestic market decreased the incentives to seek new export opportunities while

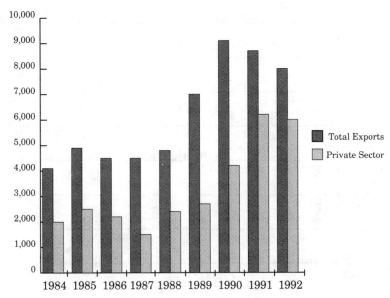

Figure 12. Nontraditional Venezuelan Exports, 1984–92
(in thousands of tons)
Source: PROMEXPORT.

uncertainty about the stability of the reforms inhibited the new invest-ments needed to restructure existing firms and make them more com-petitive internationally.

New investment in private industry, which had stagnated for most of the previous decade, also began to show strong signs of revitalization. In particular, export-oriented, natural resource-based industries attracted considerable new private foreign investment, and they are likely to account for a much larger share of Venezuelan exports in the future. It is worth noting that the book value of the total existing stock of foreign direct investment in the country at the end of 1990 was about $3.6 billion. (See figure 13.) Conservative estimates of Venezuela's attractiveness to foreign investors, which take into account the damage the political instability has done and assume that no major policy

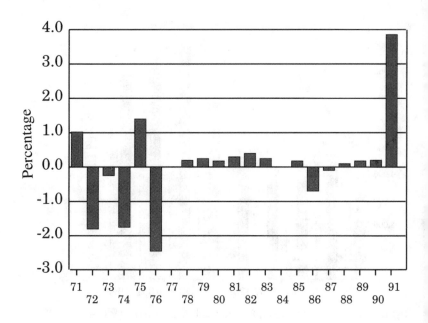

Figure 13. Net Direct Investment as a Percentage of GDP
Source: Inter-American Development Bank.

reversals to Pérez's reforms will occur, indicate that inflows of foreign investment could well exceed $10 billion during the 1990s, a sizeable boost.[19] The privatization of 40 percent of the phone company in late 1991 brought in $1.9 billion, and its planned expansion is expected to generate an additional $1 billion of annual investment in the coming years.

In 1991, confidence in the willingness and capacity of the Venezuelan government to service its foreign debt also reached unprecedented levels, driving up the price of its debt in the international secondary markets. Surprisingly, these prices were not overly affected by the political instability of 1992. After the first coup attempt, the price of the Venezuelan debt in the international secondary markets dropped. Almost immediately, however, the price recovered to levels that were equal to or higher than those of all other Latin American countries with the exception of Chile. In fact, while in February 1989 an investor could buy one dollar of Venezuelan debt for twenty-seven cents, in 1991 the cost had risen to around seventy cents. (Figure 14 shows secondary market debt prices.) Furthermore, at the end of 1991 both the government and private Venezuelan corporations had considerable success placing new debt instruments in international financial markets, a turn of events many observers would have thought impossible one or two years before.

The Balance of Payments and the Exchange Rate

During the first two years of reform, a strengthened balance of payments resulted from improved conditions—the debt renegotiation, the temporary increase in oil prices, the expansion of non-oil exports,

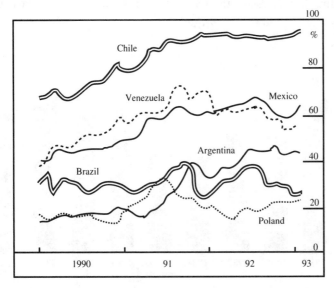

Figure 14. Secondary Market Debt Prices as a Percentage of Face Value
Source: *The Economist*, February 14, 1993.

revitalized investor confidence, the reversal of capital flight, new influxes of foreign direct investment, and only moderate increases in imports. The current account went from a $6 billion deficit in 1988 to surpluses of more than $2 billion in 1989, $8 billion in 1990, and $2.6 billion in 1991. These conditions allowed the country's gross international reserves to almost double in that period. (See figures 15 and 16.)

In 1992, the current account deteriorated to a $3.7 billion deficit as imports surged by more than 20 percent to reach their highest level in many years, while total exports remained flat. In the future, a less comfortable situation in the current account could dominate as a consequence of this trend towards higher imports (determined by trade liberalization and economic growth), the continuous decline in oil prices, and a sluggish expansion of new exports as a result of delays in overall structural reform. (See figure 17.) Political instability may continue to hamper the growth of new foreign direct investment, retarding the access to the technology and international markets also needed for steady export growth.

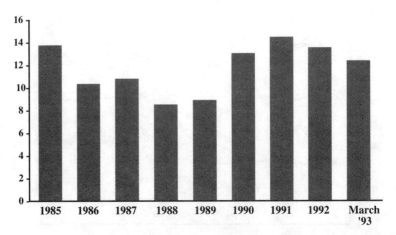

Figure 15. Venezuela—Gross Foreign Reserves (in billions of U.S. dollars)
Source: *International Financial Statistics.*

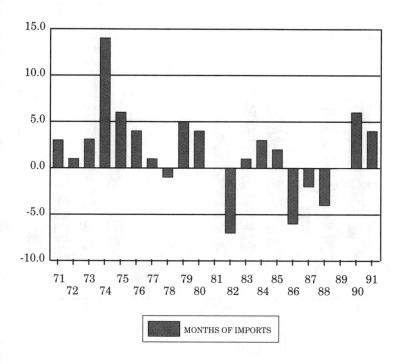

Figure 16. Change in International Reserves
Source: Inter-American Development Bank.

Closely related to these issues is the foreign exchange regime. In principle, under the regime adopted in 1989 the rate is freely determined by the supply and demand of foreign exchange. In practice, the state remains the main supplier of foreign exchange to the market by virtue of owning the oil company, the largest producer of hard currency. Every day the Central Bank sells an amount of foreign exchange calculated from the day's expected demand, the availability of other suppliers, and its reserve targets. When demand far exceeds the Central Bank's supply given its reserve targets, the bolivar undergoes a mini-devaluation. This system has sparked a great deal of political and theoretical controversy.[20] As a result, however, during the initial three

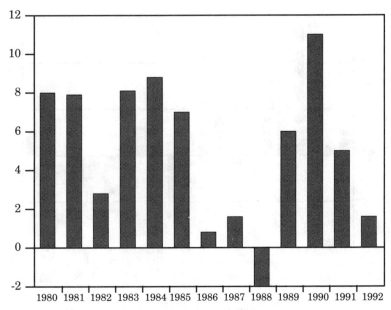

Figure 17. Trade Balance (billions of U.S. dollars)
Source: World Bank.

years of the reforms the system has achieved the lowest volatility of the currency since the fixed exchange rate system collapsed in 1983. Since the initial devaluation in 1989, the currency has adjusted rather smoothly and without the major upheavals characteristic of the period in which exchange controls held sway. (See Figure 18.) Although exporters complain that the exchange rate is overvalued, some economists argue that it is undervalued and that it feeds inflation by making imports more expensive. There is, in fact, evidence that the bolivar has been and continues to be overvalued. (Since 1980, the price of oil in real terms has decreased more than the real exchange rate.)[21] In any case, the net result has been a three-year period of enviable currency stability free of gross distortions in the price or the allocation of foreign exchange.

Nonetheless, the political pressure to return to exchange controls has never abated, and it reemerged with a vengeance in 1993, originat-

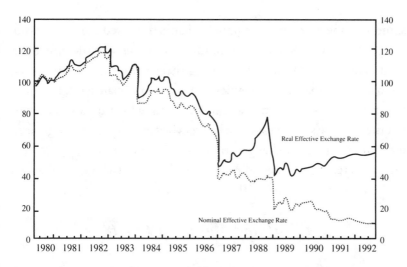

Figure 18. Venezuela—Effective Exchange Rate Indices (1980 = 100)
Source: *International Financial Statistics.*

ing primarily in the banking lobby. One unexpected aspect of the Venezuelan experience has been the difficulty of implementing reforms in the financial sector. Introducing more competition and better supervision in the financial sector turned out to be even more difficult than, for example, opening and reforming the politically sensitive agricultural sector. As a result of inadequate regulation and corruption, the portfolio of the financial sector was, in general, very feeble. Banks also tended to be severely undercapitalized. In 1992 and 1993 the fiscal deficit exerted strong inflationary pressure, and the government had to rely predominantly on tight monetary policy and high interest rates to control it. The credit squeeze, especially high interest rates, put many private companies under great strain. Many lacked adequate capital bases and had relied on the generous credits obtained through their close associations with the owners and managers of private lending institutions. At the same time, the government had begun to pay more attention to the portfolios of the financial institutions, limiting somewhat the accounting gimmicks that had masked the weakness of financial institutions' portfolios in the past. Along with the difficulties their clients began to face in servicing their debts, tighter supervision put banks and financial companies under extreme financial strain. Since lowering interest rates in the absence of capital controls would wipe out the country's reserves, some bankers began to pressure the government to reimpose exchange controls to permit a reduction of the interest rate. This is a good example of how the lack of simultaneity of the reforms undermines the entire process.

Fiscal and Monetary Effects

The results of fiscal and monetary policies are not as easy to ascertain, and there were wide swings in the first years of the reforms. While in 1989 the government achieved a solid fiscal stance, progress in the following years tended not only to lag significantly behind the general pace of improvements, but budget deficits became a serious source of instability. Delays in securing congressional approval of critical tax laws hindered many efforts at increasing public revenues and rationalizing public spending. Furthermore, during the initial two years the government failed to pay sufficient attention to the urgency of reforming the Finance Ministry. Therefore, customs reform, tax collection, the budget process, financial-sector supervision, and treasury management continued to be ignored and mismanaged. Lags in the periodic adjustments of the prices of public-sector goods also contributed to a deteriorating fiscal situation.

Current expenditures, the rigid legal framework that regulated their disbursement, and expectations of high levels of fiscal revenues spurred by the Gulf War further complicated government efforts to impose austerity in public finances.[22] Even had major efforts at restraining public spending been made, the combined impact of political pressures, institutional deficiencies, unanticipated external events, and bureaucratic inertia conspired against sounder fiscal management.

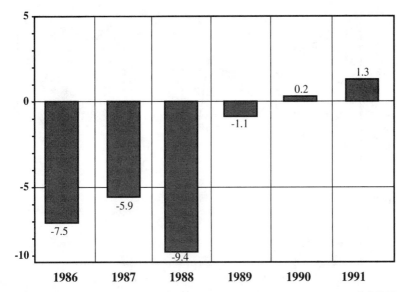

Figure 19. Public Sector Balance, 1986–91 (as a percentage of GDP)
Source: CORDIPLAN.

Nonetheless, during the first three years the fiscal situation never got out of hand and, in fact, the country could show a surplus of 1 percent of GDP in the consolidated public sector in 1989, a surplus of 0.2 percent in 1990, and—thanks to the income from privatization—a surplus equal to 1.3 percent of GDP in 1991. (See figure 19.) This was no mean showing for a country that had only recently posted a fiscal deficit of more than 9 percent of GDP.

These aggregates, however, masked a much more complex and fragile reality, such that these end results were more a function of unplanned events than of the fine-tuned management of public finances. The fact that the fiscal aggregates appeared positive also had the effect of removing the impetus for the systematic restructuring of public spending and of downgrading the reform of the Ministry of Finance from among the government's top priorities. Thus, Venezuela's chronic and profound fiscal crisis failed to merit the attention and action of the executive, Congress, or the public.

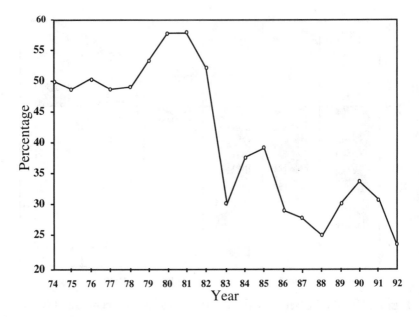

Figure 20. Public Sector Revenue (as a percentage of GDP)
Source: *International Financial Statistics.*

A complacency brought on by the initial positive results, insufficient information about the fiscal reality, an unavoidable adjustment
fatigue, a Congress staunchly opposed to the reforms, and the government's political weakness set the stage for continued delays in securing
a healthier fiscal stance. The government's weakness constrained its
capacity to increase critical public prices whose misalignment created
huge losses that negated any gains from the severe cuts it was forced
to make in other areas. The principal obstacle was the price of gasoline;
but the political impossibility of adjusting the prices of most public
utilities to levels that would, at least, recover their operating costs
greatly added to the deficit. The same was true of the losses incurred
by the operating companies of the *Corporacion Venezolana de Guayana*
(CVG), a regional holding company that owned and largely mismanaged the biggest state-owned industrial complex in the country.

The fiscal deficit resurged in 1992, reaching 6.5 percent of GDP even though the government managed to decrease public spending *in real terms*, and public-sector GDP declined 3.1 percent. Public revenues continued to lag behind needs, and private-sector income tax payments represented a paltry 1.5 percent of GDP in 1992. The government intensified negotiations with Congress over the passage of tax laws to try to correct the deficit, but the alliance of a small group of congressmen from the Christian Democratic party and *Acción Democrática* managed to sabotage all attempts at passing the value-added tax for almost four years. Not even the evidence that the fiscal cuts were threatening to further impair the already diminished capacity of the state to operate, an impending fiscal crisis of unprecedented magnitude, or pleas from their superiors in the party hierarchy could sway them from their opposition to the value-added tax.

Beyond the initial privatization initiatives and its drastic cuts in the state operating budget, the Pérez administration's efforts at restructuring the state proved ineffective, leaving major sources of fiscal waste, corruption, and inflationary spending largely intact. It seems probable that short of a reorganization and rationalization of the state modifying the patterns through which public revenue is raised and spent, the country will continue to go through these cycles of fiscal crises and painful adjustments.

In order to compensate for the fiscal deficits that began to surface again in 1990, a highly restrictive monetary policy was implemented, causing interest rates to skyrocket and to remain high in nominal terms. High real interest rates and systematic efforts to drain liquidity were the sole measures used to counter the effects of excessive public spending on the exchange rate and inflation.

Inflation

Inflation decreased sharply from its 80 percent level in 1989, dropping to 36.5 percent in 1990, and holding at about 31 percent in 1991 and in 1992. It continued to be higher than was expected or desirable.

(See figure 21.) While many hypotheses have been advanced for the inability to bring inflation below the 30 percent mark, two factors seem most significant: first is the poor coordination of fiscal and monetary policy and the failure to secure a more solid fiscal situation. Second is the persistence of oligopolistic pricing practices in a number of important industries. Although lowering tariff barriers and liberalizing imports tend to curb the pricing excesses of highly concentrated local firms, this was not the case in the initial stages of the Venezuelan reforms. Years of import substitution and promotion of domestic manufacturing coupled with price controls on end-products had stifled the development of an independent retail distribution sector. The industrial promotion scheme instead created substantial incentives for subsidized manufacturers to develop their own marketing and distribution networks. Any new imports made available by a more liberal trade regime had to be distributed through these tightly held channels.

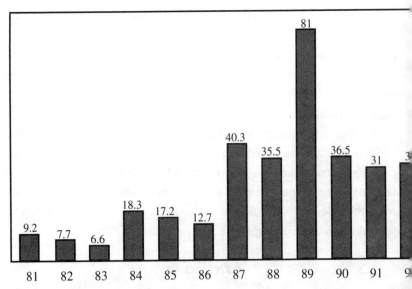

Figure 21. Inflation, 1981–91 (Percentage change in CPI)
Source: CORDIPLAN.

In practice, local manufacturers converted themselves into importing companies and utilized the same marketing channels and pricing practices in effect all along. This occurred most often in the sectors that had enjoyed more protection and were most vulnerable to competition from imports. These were also the more oligopolistic in structure and behavior. The pattern held for food, automotive parts, cars, medicines, appliances, textiles, paper, packaging and printing products, electrical and construction materials; the net effect was an increase in the consumer price index double that of the wholesale price index.[23]

In theory, new competitors and new distribution companies will erode the market power of existing firms over time, bringing about greater price competition. In practice, the entry of new competitors into the domestic distribution and retail sector will greatly depend on the existence of a business climate that makes investment attractive in industries other than those in export-oriented, resource-based areas. It has been argued that the sustained private investment activity is the last stage of adjustment and usually takes a rather long time.[24] If the Venezuelan case is typical, then economists and policymakers should revise the usual assumptions leading them to believe that trade liberalization is bound to have a substantial impact on domestic competition in the initial stages of structural reform. Moreover, the greater the impact of oligopolistic rigidities in inhibiting price competition and a decline in inflation, the longer it takes for stabilization efforts to have a beneficial effect. This, in turn, impairs the business climate and may even postpone the sort of private investment that could help introduce healthier price competition into the economy.

The Impact on the Poor and the Middle Class

Efforts to improve the social welfare of the lower and middle classes also lagged far behind needs and expectations. Prior to the reforms of 1989, generalized food subsidies and price controls had been used to cushion the impact of adverse economic conditions on the poor. However, instead of focusing the state's financial efforts on those who genuinely needed financial assistance, these constituted a very inefficient subsidy to the general population and even to neighboring countries. A can of powdered milk or sardines had the same artificially low price for the wife of a wealthy business executive, a destitute pregnant mother in a slum, or a speculator who smuggled the goods to Colombia. Not surprisingly, a World Bank study found that the poor consumed only 40 percent of the goods that the government subsidized at an enormous cost. The rest were consumed by the middle or upper classes, used by industry, or exported.[25]

In the past, any efforts to channel needed goods and services to specific vulnerable groups were immediately transformed by the party in power into an instrument to build electoral support and reward party members. This capture of social programs by political parties severely stunted the development of organizational capacities in the agencies in charge of delivering social services. Together with their domination by their unions, this political domination made social agencies highly corrupt and inefficient. This partly explains why Venezuela had poverty indicators worse than those of much poorer countries despite spending 40 percent of its budget and 10 to 14 percent of GDP in the social sectors in the 1970s, the highest per capita social expenditure in Latin America.

Unemployment underwent no major surges during the initial years, and after 1989 it decreased steadily, reaching around 7 percent in 1992. Furthermore, after more than a decade of continuous deterioration, real salaries also began to recover. Despite these positive results, basic living standards had suffered from the elimination of subsidies and price controls. Also, the reduction in real terms of the public-sector budget reduced the quality and availability of public services, creating additional difficulties for the poor.

The new social programs that directly targeted the poor were put into effect, and by 1990 an additional 1 percent of GDP per year was devoted to them. Small, labor-intensive infrastructure projects designed to alleviate unemployment were launched as well. The critical problem, however, was not high unemployment or a dearth of resources for the social sectors.[26] Instead, all social service delivery systems had, in fact, collapsed or were performing at their minimum capacity: the health and education ministries and the agencies in charge of providing housing, food aid, or maternal and child care for the poor had barely functioned even while receiving huge budget allocations. As these became tighter and demand for their services grew because of the crisis, what little capacity remained eroded further and in some cases disappeared altogether. (Figure 22 shows investment in public services.)

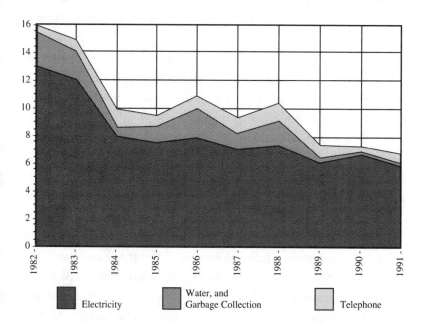

Figure 22. Investment in Public Services, 1982–91 (Billions of bolivars, 1984 = 100)
Source: CORDIPLAN.

Public hospitals, for example, lacked reliable controls to avoid the periodic disappearance of materials and medical equipment; every few years they had to be completely re-equipped, from beds to x-ray machines. Inventory management was primitive or nonexistent. The standard practice to guarantee the minimum necessary supply of medicine was massive overstocking, thus making the apparent consumption per capita of some medicines among the highest in the world. Attempts at correcting these problems were systematically resisted by the medical and paramedical unions. They held the government hostage with the threat of paralyzing the public health system. In addition, the businesses and individuals that extracted huge profits from the corrupt procurement system, the lack of trained managers capable of running a modern hospital, and the inability of the state to attract and retain the few who were available in the country made institutional reform almost impossible. These circumstances have made medical travesties a commonplace: most patients, regardless of medical condition or socioeconomic status, are treated only after they have privately procured their own medical supplies; Venezuelan vaccination rates are half the Latin American average despite per capita health expenditures that are the second highest in the region.

The basic characteristics of the situation in medicine—congestion, waste, corruption, mismanagement, politicization, regressiveness, lack of trained personnel, misguided unionism, and labor laws that made change almost impossible—pertained in almost all social service delivery institutions.

The Pérez administration was very conscious of its political isolation, the country's institutional weakness, and the socially and politically destabilizing effects that the reforms were having. Along with the rest of the country, public officials were shocked and disturbed by the riots that met the first policy changes. These factors, combined with Pérez's historical ties to the labor movement and the apparent willingness of some labor leaders to avoid an open confrontation with the administration, led the government to postpone any attempt at liberalizing labor laws and practices. The government likewise avoided a confrontation with the unions over control of public agencies. The ministries of education and health are the largest employers in the country, and as such they have the largest and most powerful unions. These unions, in turn, are dominated by political parties. For many years, union leaders in social-sector agencies, public utilities such as water and sanitation, or services such as public transportation enjoyed more power and stability than the titular heads of the agencies.

It is easy to imagine that a government that felt constantly under fire and that lacked any significant political support would be very careful not to provoke a general strike that would paralyze indefinitely the country's hospitals, public transportation, schools, or universities. So while the government attempted to bargain with public-sector unions over salaries and other conditions, it did very little to ease the hold of the union elites on the functioning of public agencies.

The administration was even forced to accept a new labor law sponsored by Rafael Caldera, a former president, who had it passed almost single-handedly in 1990. Caldera's law was a clear relapse into the worst excesses of populism and contrasted starkly with the direction most other countries were taking in terms of labor legislation. Moreover, it was in basic contradiction to the reforms the government was implementing. Nonetheless, President Pérez decided not to exercise his veto, which would only have delayed the law's passage for a few months while creating yet another source of political unrest.

The government's incapacity—or unwillingness—to confront the task of freeing the public agencies in charge of crucial social services from the grip of the highly corrupt unions helped prepare the ground for the violent attacks the administration eventually endured. For most Venezuelans, such stark realities as the absence of a reliable social safety net, the near-collapse of social services, the deterioration of public utilities and services (water, sanitation, telephone, electricity, transportation, and police), and persistent price increases canceled out any benefits that might eventually accrue from the successes in terms of balance of payments or economic growth. These were but remote abstractions for very large segments of society.

These social problems had accumulated over several decades and alleviating them would inevitably take time. But Venezuelans had expected that their sacrifices would be rapidly compensated by an improvement in living standards. Although, in all probability, standards of living would have declined even farther in the absence of corrective actions, in terms of public opinion things could not have been worse. The extremely slow progress in the institutional reconstruction of social services in the first years of the reform program was certainly not a satisfactory answer to ever more desperate living conditions— a fact with significant political repercussions.

The Private Sector: From Courting the State to Courting the Market

Never before in history had the Venezuelan government placed so much faith in and transferred so much responsibility to the private sector as during the reforms launched in 1989. Price liberalization, privatization, trade reform, easing of controls on foreign direct investment, deregulation of entire sectors, and even the reliance on private nongovernmental organizations to provide social services made market mechanisms, entrepreneurship, and private investment the critical factors for the success of the government's development strategy. One critical risk of such reforms is to burden the private sector with so many hopes, expectations, and responsibilities that frustration and disappointment are bound to result. Such frustration may set the stage for a political backlash that make such reforms more difficult to sustain.

The Venezuelan experience shows that the form, speed, intensity, and effects of the private sector's response to market-oriented reforms is very difficult to anticipate with any degree of precision. For instance, the amount of flight capital available for repatriation is less than what has fled over the years. This certainly constitutes a sound base on which the private sector can rapidly build a new and enlarged role. But, as the Venezuelan example shows, it is a mistake to assume that these funds will all be available for repatriation simply as a result of a more attractive environment for private investment.

Some Venezuelans own large amounts of capital deposited abroad, and it seems safe to assume that a portion of that capital is available for investments within the country. The facts seem to bear this out— in the first years of reforms, more capital entered the country than left it. Nevertheless, the ownership structure of this capital generates impediments to its mobility that limit the amount that will be available for investment within the country in the medium term.

Specifically, we must assume that there is a portion of foreign assets belonging to former public officials, politicians, union leaders, and others whose owners cannot justifiably lay claim to it. For these "underground capitalists," investing within the country carries the risk of exposing their ties to assets acquired under questionable circumstances—a higher than normal risk. Only projects with rates of return capable of compensating these additional risks will be attractive to them. Such projects are not common. And should that criterion be met, the investment vehicle would also have to assure complete anonymity to investors, concealing their identities as the owners of these funds. A final impediment to repatriation of these foreign holdings is attitude: these individuals, rather than being businessmen are rentiers, lacking in the entrepreneurial outlook and skills needed to identify and structure their participation in a business venture.

The other segment of the population with significant flight-capital holdings is the business community. Obstacles to capital repatriation exist here as well. The new conditions created by the market-oriented reforms require a different set of business talents from the ones that worked under the past regime of protection, subsidies, and restricted competition. While a new generation of more aggressive and competitive entrepreneurs is emerging and taking advantage of the new opportunities, the ability of many businesses to turn a profit under heightened domestic and international competition has simply wasted away. Given the risk-return relationship of their foreign holdings versus those for direct investments in the country over the short term (and possibly even the medium term) business has shied away from capital repatriation for purposes of direct investment. The chairman of an important business group in Venezuela expressed this bias candidly.

> Since we began business in the early sixties, the government had always protected and offered us all sorts of special incentives. It's true that it also controlled our prices and made life difficult in many other ways, but on balance it created conditions for us and others to grow and prosper. We never had to worry a whole lot about foreign competition, and the exchange rate made it impossible for us to even attempt to export. From the start, exports had never been a government priority, and for thirty years it was obvious that creating employment and supplying the local markets was all that was expected from us.

> Now all of a sudden the new government tells us not only that interest rates will be three times higher and that the price we pay for electricity will increase threefold, but that the protection against cheaper foreign products will be taken away from us and that we will have to be able to compete internationally and start exporting. In order to do that I will have to do two things. One is to bring back [repatriate] several million dollars, buy new machinery, and modernize our operation, making it more efficient. And the other is to buy myself and my people new suitcases and start traveling around the world trying to sell my products in competition with the Taiwanese and the Koreans, who, by the way, have been doing it for decades before us. On top of all this of course, I will be risking the possibility that a new government, or even a new team in this same government, will change policies and let the exchange rate appreciate and wipe out any competitive gains that we may have achieved.

> At the same time, our holdings abroad not only are safe and without risks in comparison to our local operations, but each year they generate more profits than we can ever dream of making here, and this without having to worry about the government, the unions, or the Taiwanese. . . .[27]

These attitudes illustrate what is perhaps one of the most damaging and least examined side-effects of capital flight—the neutering of the entrepreneurial impulses of a segment of the private sector. Capital flight transformed most entrepreneurs into rentiers with little interest in the challenges of building a new business under the difficult political and economic circumstances typical of a developing country. Why run the risk of starting up a new factory if the rent of capital invested overseas provides an effortless and comparatively more stable return in hard currency? Additionally, in most developing countries, the number of firms with the entrepreneurial resources—capital, organization, technology, and so forth—needed to pursue new business initiatives is quite limited. Of these few, those that have retained their entrepreneurial spirit and are actively pursuing new opportunities face organizational obstacles to the expansion of their scope of operations. While access to capital may not be a problem, the availability of organizational support imposes limits on the speed and extent to which they may utilize available capital and exploit the new opportunities created by the reforms.

These considerations confirm the importance of reliable, efficient, and transparent capital markets and stock markets for the freer return of flight capital. Along with a judicial system that consistently upholds contracts and property rights, these are the fundamental elements of the enabling environment for private investment. Yet they may still be insufficient to attract local private investors. Opportunities are also required, and under the new policy framework these will be attractive only to companies with a substantial degree of competitiveness. Firms have to be capable of successfully competing with imports, with foreign firms in the local market, or with world players in the international markets. Since so few Venezuelan corporations have been required to hone such competitive skills, in the near term new business initiatives will have to rely heavily on foreign companies that have the needed technology, marketing skills, and access to international markets. Once again, direct foreign investment emerges as a critical catalyst for the economic restructuring of reforming countries.

The Venezuelan experience is also interesting vis-à-vis the debate over the extent and the nature of the direct support that the state should provide to specific industries. In this debate, one school of thought uses the success of Japan and the East Asian NICs (newly industrializing countries) as an example of the positive role that the state has played in support of the private sector. It contends that the strong export performance of these countries was achieved by targeting specific industrial sectors and channeling a plethora of subsidies and incentives to private firms therein. These sectors also enjoyed the sustained attention of an active set of government agencies working in close partnership.[28] The opposing view stresses that in many countries where the government selected priority industrial sectors, this only served to make a small number of entrepreneurs and their friends in government very rich, and in fact, eventually weakened competitiveness.[29]

The results of Venezuela's three years of reform indicate that a targeted industrial policy was neither feasible nor desirable. In the first place, the government clearly lacked the political autonomy to enact an industrial policy based on an objective, independent selection of priority sectors. The government had stretched its political capital to the limit trying to sustain its reforms. The conflicts among some of the big conglomerates were already causing political instability. Given the small number of controlling parties in the private sector, announcing that the government would proceed to choose priority industries for support was equivalent to taking sides with the conglomerate that dominated the particular sector. Any such action would invite repercussions from those left out, adding to political instability.

Even assuming that the government had the autonomy needed to withstand the political manipulations of these powerful actors, advocates of targeted industrial policies in Venezuela and abroad have not yet proposed coherent objective criteria to guide the selection process. And even if these existed, the government lacked basic statistical information about performance on which any transparent selection of a country's export leaders would be based. The Venezuelan state had never relied on sound information to manage the economy, and it therefore lacked a dependable system for the collection and analysis of economic data. Moreover, during the initial stages of macroeconomic stabilization policies and structural reforms, all economic variables and parameters were in constant flux, making reliable assessments almost impossible early in the process. These factors added to the likelihood that industrial policy would fall prey to the influence of private conglomerates, which are more powerful and permanent than many economic ministers or even presidents.

The difficulties of bestowing a differential treatment on individual industries were rapidly discerned by the Pérez government when it began to prepare its trade reform package. It was soon evident that neither the president nor those in charge of the reforms had any hope of politically surviving a process in which all industries—that is, all economic conglomerates—were not treated equally. Thus, the government's ability to eliminate tariff protections and subsidies to the private sector was due, in large measure, to the fact that it was done transparently and indiscriminately, affecting every industrial sector equally. The government successfully resisted competing demands for special treatment thanks to its strong commitment to neutrality. Here too, any selection of specific industries for concessions regarding trade liberalization would have ended up being more a function of political influence than of real or potential competitiveness.

The impossibility of implementing industrial policies in which the state plays a more active role does not mean that the problems of industrial development that inspire such policies did not surface in Venezuela. Venezuelan firms that actively pursued export strategies encountered great difficulty in entering foreign markets regardless of how competitive they were. Even in the case of a relatively open country, the United States, the Venezuelan exports that were stimulated by the new policy orientation were blocked by fourteen different legal actions on behalf of U.S. firms seeking to protect their markets. While some of these actions were overruled by the GATT or by U.S. courts, these actions alone cost Venezuelan firms an estimated $400 million per year in lost potential earnings.[30] Exports to other markets are being hampered by subtle and outright protectionist practices in many countries, or they are beaten out by other firms that enjoy a competitive advantage due to experience, greater resources, or the effective support of their governments. Meanwhile, as the domestic economy recovers its import capacity and tariff protection continues its scheduled decline, allegations by local producers about international dumping in Venezuela are heard with increasing frequency.

Probably the single most important constraint the private sector faces in fulfilling the promise on which much of the reform effort is predicated lies in the mismatch between the human resources needed to compete internationally and those that the country's educational system turns out. International experience shows that a country's gains in competitiveness are usually preceded by concerted efforts at professional education and vocational training.[31] In Venezuela, as in many other countries in the region, the decrepit state of public universities and training centers greatly hinders such efforts. Their condition is not due to lack of funds. Venezuela boasts the highest per capita expenditure in public education in Latin America, and 55 percent of education spending goes to higher education (which has only 7.5 percent of total student enrollment).[32] Universities fall prey to the same problems of congestion, clientelism, isolation, and mismanagement that plague other social institutions. Unions and other internal groups have effectively resisted changes that threaten their long established domination. Any attempt at developing a constructive relationship between higher education offerings and the training needed to enhance international competitiveness hinges on the government's ability to minimize the interference of these groups.

In sum, major unresolved questions exist as to how to reconcile the political, technical, and institutional limitations of providing Venezuelan private firms with the direct government support most of their international competitors enjoy without returning to past practices when targeting industries stultified the competitive drive.

Given these circumstances, two main factors dominated business's initial reaction to the new policies. First was the need to rapidly improvise business strategies to deal with unforeseen and unprecedented circumstances that threatened their survival. While for years business had demanded the adoption of market-based policies, few firms really believed that such an approach would ever be taken. Consequently, private firms were woefully unprepared to deal with the consequences of these policies and the many dislocations that typically accompany their implementation. Fortunately, most of these firms had been born and bred in a highly unstable business environment where market conditions and government policies changed often and dramatically. Hence, companies did not lack in the management skills, organizational capabilities, and resources needed to adjust to profound changes in their business environment.

Secondly, the institutional arrangements through which the private sector had interacted with the state in the past became obsolete practically overnight. The formal network of business councils, chambers of commerce, and the assorted associations representing business were hard pressed to devise timely and adequate responses to the new situation. The environment in which they had specialized for most of their existence no longer needed their services. Bargaining with public bureaucrats for foreign exchange allocations, prices, import or export quotas, and even publicly denouncing the inadequacy of the government's interventionist policies was no longer necessary. However, the possibilities for free agents—businessmen or their representatives who extracted special concessions for companies by circumventing the formal, corporatist, institutional setting of the private sector—also diminished as a result of the loss of discretionary power on the part of government officials.

The private sector's influence over the government was also constrained by the government's swift action in so many different policy areas at the same time. This reduced the opportunities for the private-sector actors to steer the policies towards the interests of any specific group or industry. Moreover, the very nature of the policies, with their intention of creating a level playing field for all participants and eliminating special privileges for specific sectors obviously helped buffer government officials and their policies from the particular groups that fought to retain the privileges they had enjoyed for decades.[33]

As immediate consequences of the initial decisions taken by the Pérez administration, all costs rose dramatically and demand dwindled to levels that had not been seen for years creating a very threatening situation for most private firms. In consumer durables, for instance, sales plunged. After having had years in which two hundred thousand new cars were sold, the automotive sector hit a record low in 1989 selling fewer than forty thousand units. The 10 percent drop in GDP, a devaluation of almost 200 percent, an inflation level that surpassed 80 percent, and a decline in real salaries of 20 percent put the cash flows of most private companies under tremendous, unprecedented strain.

Furthermore, most companies were being choked by the massive inventories they had accumulated in 1988 in anticipation of the devaluation that any administration inaugurated in 1989 had, inevitably, to impose. These inventories were financed locally at the subsidized high negative interest rates determined by the government. Once the new administration eliminated controls on interest rates, they shot up, rising 150 percent. Freeing the interest rate and allowing it to reach levels consistent with inflation ended a long era in which gross financial distortions were allowed to accumulate. Government policies had created all sorts of incentives for private companies to be undercapitalized and financially overextended, while their shareholders could amass funds that were normally deposited abroad in private accounts. After the reforms, real interest rates made it financially unbearable for the highly leveraged firms to carry large inventories.

For most private firms, however, the biggest threat during the initial years of the reforms arose from the government-imposed requirement to partially refinance $6 billion in letters of credit associated with the massive imports they had made in 1988. At that time, the government encouraged—and in some cases, it even required—that imports be financed by letters of credit for which it guaranteed the foreign exchange rate. Once the exchange rate was allowed to float and to depreciate by more than 150 percent, the government was faced with the difficult decision of whether to use public funds to cover the foreign exchange losses stemming from the guarantees issued to importers by the previous administration. Honoring such commitments would propel the fiscal deficit to levels that would bring on hyperinflation.

The government decided to transfer part of these losses to the private companies that had incurred them, imposing further pressures on their already negative cash flows.[34] Private-sector exports soared to an all-time high in a frenzied bid to acquire foreign exchange. Private companies that had exported $649 worth of goods in 1988 exported more than $1.5 billion in 1989. Companies re-exported inputs and (to a much lesser extent) machinery that they had imported a few months earlier. But the bulk of exports consisted of the manufactured goods for which companies could not find buyers locally. Furthermore, an attractive exchange rate and a sizable and ill-conceived export subsidy made companies all the more aggressive in seeking ways to sell their local production abroad. Some even utilized the criminal skills honed in a decade of corruption-prone government intervention and claimed the export subsidy by falsifying records and bribing public officials to exaggerate export sales or even create nonexistent ones.

The other means through which private companies dealt with their cash-flow problems in 1989 was simple, effective and, for most of them, unprecedented: shareholders repatriated some of the funds they had abroad. In fact, that year about $1 billion entered the country, a sizable portion of which went to support financially strapped firms.

Another major change that companies had to digest was the most comprehensive trade reform in the nation's history. To the surprise of many observers, the massive wave of bankruptcies brought on by local manufacturers' inability to compete with cheaper and better imports never came about. The exchange rate provided sufficient price protection, and Venezuela's retail sector lacked the vigor and acumen needed to exploit the import opportunities created by the trade reforms. Many years of government preference for the expansion of the manufacturing base had constrained the development of an independent retail sector. Thus, while private firms had to endure severe hardships in the initial years of the reforms, very few filed for bankruptcy. Companies were restructured, changed, capitalized, bought, sold, and merged. Rarely, however, did they go out of business altogether.

The liberalization of foreign investment in early 1990 also had major repercussions for the local business sector. On the one hand, the fact that foreign firms could now freely invest and operate in the country (even in sectors that had been previously off-limits) represented new and very threatening competition for local firms. On the other hand, a liberalized and more welcoming environment for foreign companies also created many new opportunities for local firms. The technology, marketing skills, and access to export markets that foreigners brought with them could now be coupled with whatever resources and skills local companies might have, allowing both to profit from the many opportunities left untapped over the years of isolation and economic decay.

The deregulation of foreign investment was extended to the stock market, where for the first time foreigners were allowed to own local securities. The Caracas stock market, the most significant in the country, was comparatively small (138 companies were listed in 1991). Emerging from its primitive and dormant state, it became the center of feverish activity. In 1990, no other stock market in the world performed better in real dollar terms.[35] Closely held companies which but a few months earlier would not have even considered the possibility of utilizing the stock market to raise capital or float their debt instruments could no longer afford to ignore such alternatives. Stock market activity was also spurred by a series of takeovers, some of them hostile.[36] In 1991 the boom tended to level off—growth was 34 percent in U.S. dollars. Unfortunately, since portfolio investment is notoriously sensitive to signs of instability, and these were considerable in Venezuela in 1992, the stock market plunged 40 percent in that year.

In general, reforms did revitalize the private sector. Private capital was partially repatriated, new export-oriented companies were created, and foreign investment increased. Public companies were privatized and became important investors as they expanded and modernized their operations, closely held companies widened their ownership through the stock market, inefficient companies had to streamline their operations, and financial markets became more active than ever. But perhaps the most important change was that private companies had found new reasons to invest time and money in becoming more competitive and to direct their concerns toward better serving the needs of consumers instead of being obsessed by the whims of bureaucrats and politicians.

But not all of the structural changes in the private sector have been positive. Concentration of ownership seems to have increased, and the extreme deficiencies of the regulatory framework for business combined with the institutional weaknesses of the agencies in charge of enforcing regulations have allowed significant distortions to emerge. The portfolios of most banks largely consist of loans to affiliate companies or to other private businesses owned by their shareholders and directors. Moreover, there is mounting evidence that, in many cases the quality of such portfolios is extremely low and that the capitalization of most banks is grossly insufficient to cover the potentially enormous losses. Bank supervision in Venezuela has historically been weak and nothing indicates that it has escaped the propensity for corruption typical of public bureaucracies in charge of dealing with the private sector. The same applies to the *Comision Nacional de Valores* (the agency in charge of regulating the stock market), the public agencies in charge of enforcing environmental protection laws, and those in charge of ensuring compliance by radio and television stations with state licensing rules.

Other public agencies crucial to the healthy development of a strong and competitive private sector were created only in 1992 and are still in their infancy. This is true of the agencies in charge of enforcing consumer protection, antitrust, and antidumping laws. It is also the case for the public agencies responsible for regulating utilities that have been or are in the process of being privatized. As owner of the telephone company, the state never needed the independent regulatory capacity it needs now that the phone company is in private hands. With the privatization of the airlines, water, electricity, garbage collection, hospitals, public transportation, toll roads, and many other public services, the demands for regulatory services are growing much faster than the state's capacity to provide them. Unfortunately, it is a safe bet that this regulatory gap will be the source of many future scandals, and of much political attention and public dissatisfaction.

Another unexpected result of the 1989 reforms were the takeovers and oligopolistic wars that broke out among the economic conglomerates in the private sector. The competition introduced by the reforms upset the delicate equilibrium between rival groups, itself the result of years of intermittent wars, collusion, and market-sharing agreements. Whenever competition appeared, it seldom expressed itself through prices or other marketing tactics, all of which had been inhibited by the interventionist policies of the government. Instead groups competed by trying to control the supply of raw materials and other inputs or the financing and distribution channels. Therefore, rivalries were essentially directed at gaining control of certain strategically placed companies that would in turn ensure greater control, protection, or influence over the actions of other companies contending in the same markets.[37]

Once the policies restricting competition were lifted, most companies entered into an oligopolistic frenzy, trying to amass additional strategic holdings and to block the advances of their rivals. Other moves by large firms, however, turned very nasty and became an additional source of political instability.

The implications of these trends for the future evolution of democratic processes in Venezuela are as worrisome as their ramifications for the evolution of a more competitive private sector. How these trends develop will be closely entwined with the direction the political situation takes and with the state's struggle to gain sufficient independence to promote greater competition.

Chapter 6
The Coups and
Their Political Aftermath

The day after attending a conference in Switzerland, the president flew back to Venezuela, arriving at the airport the evening of Monday, February 3, 1992. To his surprise, the defense minister was waiting for him at the gate, and an unprecedented array of soldiers stood guard. The minister informed Pérez that he had taken military control of the airport as a precaution against an attack by rebellious units within the army. The army's counterintelligence directorate had notified him of an impending attack against the president upon his return from Switzerland.[38]

The president's motorcade left the airport, stopped briefly at the official residence, *La Casona*, then drove to *Miraflores*, the presidential palace, located at the opposite end of Caracas. Between midnight and 1:00 A.M. on February 4, a group of heavily armed soldiers backed by armored vehicles started to attack *Miraflores*. Other rebel units attacked *La Casona* and the nearby Francisco de Miranda air base, the site of air force headquarters. Rebel troops also attempted (unsuccessfully) to take over the headquarters of the government intelligence services but did manage to blockade army and navy headquarters and the Ministry of Defense.

President Pérez barely escaped being killed or captured by the rebels by exiting the palace through a back door and hiding under a coat in the back seat of an unmarked car. He traveled to a private television station where he contacted loyal army chiefs and managed to broadcast a speech to the nation. In it, he explained that an attempt on his life had taken place but that except for a small group of rebels, the armed forces remained loyal to the Constitution and, thereby, to him, as president and commander-in-chief. He emphasized that the coup could not succeed, that loyal forces were regaining control of the situation, and that he had received calls from U.S. President Bush, most Latin American presidents, and other world leaders expressing solidarity and full support for his government.

One of the major blunders of the coup was that the rebels failed to gain control over radio and television stations or public utilities such as power and telephone service. In fact, rebel soldiers went to one of the private television stations only to discover that its broadcasting facilities had been moved to another location more than three years earlier. Another group of soldiers took over the public television station and asked to broadcast a message to the nation that their leaders had taped on videocassette. The president of the station convinced the officer in charge of the group that the format of their videotape was incompatible with the station's and that it would take some time to arrange for its conversion to broadcast format. This subterfuge stalled the request long enough for loyal forces to gain control. Broadcast of the taped message would have obviously undermined the impact that Pérez gained by virtue of the fact that his and his supporters' public announcements were the only ones made during the events. Had the rebels gained operational control of at least some radio and television stations, events might have unfolded quite differently.

The president was soon joined at the television station by Eduardo Fernandez, the secretary general of the Christian Democrats, the main opposition party. At 2:30 A.M. Fernandez went on the air with an impassioned speech stating that though he too opposed the government, the only acceptable way of expressing opposition was through democratic means. The president spoke again later to inform the nation that most rebel forces had surrendered and exhorted those few still fighting to give up. The heads of the other main political parties, the workers' federation (CTV) and the private-sector federation (FED-ECAMARAS), also appeared on television to condemn the uprising and express support for democracy and constitutional rule. At 5:00

A.M., President Pérez went back on the air, this time from *Miraflores* palace to inform the public that his government had complete control of the situation and that all the leaders of the revolt were under arrest.

Just as in the February 1989 riots, Pérez convened his cabinet and passed a decree suspending constitutional guarantees. While reviewing the situation with his ministers that morning, the defense minister, General Fernando Ochoa repeatedly requested authorization to let the arrested coup leader, 38-year-old Lt. Col. Hugo Chávez, appear on television to ask rebel holdouts in different parts of the country to surrender to avoid further bloodshed. The president had already refused to negotiate with the rebels, even at one point vehemently informing the defense minister, "I do not want negotiations of any kind General, give them bullets. . .!!!" Just before noon, Pérez granted permission to broadcast a videotaped, edited message from Chávez. Instead, Defense Minister Ochoa allowed Chávez to appear live in a nationally broadcast message that contributed more to destabilizing Venezuelan democracy in two minutes than all the shots fired through the night. Impeccably dressed in uniform, showing no sign of fatigue or stress, Chávez delivered a short speech, first emphasizing his Bolivarian values, then stating:

> Unfortunately, *for now*, the objectives we sought were not achieved in the capital city. That is, we in Caracas could not take control of power. You, there in the interior, did a great job. But it is time now to avoid further bloodshed; it is time to reflect. We will have new situations. The country definitely has to embark on the road to a better destiny.[39]

Chávez accepted full responsibility for the uprising and stated that he was prepared to bear the consequences of his actions. He was a compelling and uncommon sight for television viewers accustomed to the verbal and political maneuverings of traditional politicians: a public figure who acknowledged that he personally had failed while others had done a great job; who maintained an unfaltering position even after failure and defeat; who faced responsibility and did not try to evade the repercussions of his actions. His televised image conveyed the possibility of change, a break from the political and economic schemes usually blamed for the country's problems. A new face unrelated to the traditional power structures and offering to guide the nation back to prosperity, equality, and integrity was an item that, regardless of its packaging, was bound to appeal to a mass audience. That the item was, in fact, a primitive army tyrant was easily concealed by the illusion that any change meant progress.

But Chávez's televised address was not the only one. Rafael Caldera, president from 1968 to 1973 and founder of the Christian Democratic party (COPEI), also took advantage of the situation to promote his views. On the afternoon of February 4, Congress met in emergency session to consider the cabinet's request for the temporary suspension of constitutional guarantees (which it eventually approved). All major political parties had agreed to support it, and no speeches were scheduled. Caldera, one of the founding fathers of Venezuelan democracy, unexpectedly requested the opportunity to address the session, which was being broadcast by the official television and radio stations and retransmitted by all others. Caldera proceeded to deliver a message that left congressmen shocked, the government bewildered, and his popularity ratings soaring. He briefly condemned the takeover by force then proceeded to detail how the rebels' motives were amply justified by the country's situation. He insisted that the economic policies that had left Venezuelans so poor and in such miserable conditions were a sacrifice that no one had the right to demand in the name of democracy. He concluded by asking President Pérez to "rectify" his economic program.

From then on, the political situation for Pérez and his government deteriorated rapidly and continuously. As one observer noted, the government was retroactively "kidnapped" by Chávez and Caldera with the unexpected assistance of its own television cameras.

Why Did the First Coup Fail?

Paradoxically, and in contrast to the February 1989 riots, when several weeks passed before normalcy began to emerge, the events of February 1992 caused no major interruption of Venezuelans' day-to-day routines. The day after the coup, economic life proceeded as usual, with shops, businesses, schools, and government offices open and functioning as if nothing had happened. The same was not true of the political system, however. While the coup failed to unseat the government, it managed to provoke the deepest political crisis the country had faced since democracy was restored in 1958.

The leaders of the failed coup were four lieutenant colonels.[40] All were well known among their colleagues for their negative view of the current form of Venezuelan democracy and for their outspoken criticism of the way in which the national leadership—including that of the armed forces—was running the country. The four referred repeatedly to the ideas and writings of Simon Bolivar; they insisted that the ruling classes' corruption had to be stopped by any means and that the armed forces should prevent politicians from bargaining away Venezuela's rights to Colombia (in the two countries' century-old border dispute).[41]

As it was later discovered, the leaders of the coup had some regular contact with the small civilian groups from the radical left that had remained active since the guerilla wars of the 1960s. These groups were expected to play an important role in mobilizing popular support in the barrios and universities once the revolt was under way in the morning. These street actions, however, did not have much chance to take hold given that the revolt had already failed by then.

The coup's failure was due to the many mistakes and fundamental oversights of its leaders, to President Pérez's instincts and quick reactions, and to his exclusive access to radio and television during the night of the attack. The lack of active participation by the population and other units of the armed forces, which the rebels had hoped for, was also an important factor. While rebel forces were able to enter the capital, attack, and capture certain strategic sites in Caracas as well as the cities of Maracaibo, Maracay, and Valencia, a relatively small number of army units took active part in the uprising.

Major errors committed within the armed forces and other government security agencies made the rebel officers' actions of much greater consequence than they would have otherwise been. As noted, the leaders of the uprising were well known, and rumors about their intentions had been circulating for years. They held planning meetings with a minimum of caution, and the day before the uprising higher echelons within the army had information about the plans and largely ignored it.[42] The rebels entered Caracas on a main highway in daylight by bus. Although heavily armed and undisguised, they triggered none of the warning mechanisms a state or army normally has. These facts may be seen as evidence of general complicity within the military with the plotters. There are indications that other groups within the military led the plotters to believe that they would join in the uprising. When it became evident that Pérez had escaped alive and that he was the only one on television, that he had the support of several military battalions, that people did not take to the streets to support the rebels, and that the coup had little chance of succeeding, these other groups not only failed to support the rebels but even obeyed orders to attack them.

But the failure to anticipate the uprising at an earlier stage and prevent it does not seem to have been the result of any extensive involvement of the armed forces in the conspiracy. More to the point, the complacency bred over years of relative stability along with the advanced institutional decay characteristic of the Venezuelan state undermined the armed forces capacity to react effectively to an attempt to topple an elected government. Furthermore, the media had been repeating largely unfounded rumors of an imminent coup since the beginning of the Pérez administration, a factor bound to have dampened the alertness of intelligence and state security apparatus. In sum, the fact that the armed forces are part and parcel of a greatly weakened state in which authority and efficiency are but rare phenomena should be taken into consideration in any assessment of their involvement in this event.

Explanations of the coup that stress its economic, social, and political determinants are valid. However, the coup would have never occurred—or its impact would have been far less—had the state not lost the capacity to perform even the most rudimentary security services needed to ensure its own survival. These events were staged by four rather isolated individuals able to persuade or coerce only a small number of their peers into joining them; the state acted only after the seats of power were under bombardment.

The Aftermath: A Political Hangover

The uprising, together with Caldera's and Chávez's speeches, galvanized disparate classes and parties in opposition to Pérez and his government. Any inhibition to protest crumbled as formerly passive social groups and respectable individuals vocally expressed dissatisfaction with a government that not only pursued widely unpopular policies but also, in their view, jeopardized Venezuela's democratic stability. Other events conspired as well—the possibility of another military coup was not completely dispelled, Pérez appeared weak, and his party, *Acción Democrática*, failed to support him decisively during the night of the coup. These precipitated a wave of political attacks on the president, culminating in calls for his resignation from all camps—labor unions, the private sector, the public bureaucracy, all political parties, professional associations, university professors, students, farmers, the armed forces, media owners, the middle class, and, in general, almost any nameable sector and group of society. Each had either experienced a lowering of its standard of living or lost some privilege during the reforms of the Pérez administration. Never—until the coup—had their convergence been possible.

Certain traditional factions within the political parties led the call for a radical reversal of economic policy. Others insisted the crisis was political and ethical in nature, and that the concentration of power in the traditional political parties had bred the widespread corruption that permeated all of society. Many causes were found; most were eventually reduced to President Pérez, blaming him for his pursuit of painful economic policies and for his indecisiveness in the fight against corruption.

To survive, the government needed to broaden its base of support and promote a number of political and institutional reforms. Pérez consulted intensively with a wide variety of groups and individuals and took action on several different fronts. The prevailing political uncertainty was dizzying, and institutional instability reached new lows. Early on Pérez had failed to recruit into his cabinet individuals representing a broad spectrum of political perspectives and interests. He now appointed such a diverse group to the newly created, largely ineffective, and short-lived State Council, which was to have an advisory role. Later the president was successful in persuading the Christian Democrats to join the government. Their response gives a good idea of the confusion reigning at the time: the party decided to join the government but only by authorizing two of its members to join the cabinet in a private capacity and not as party representatives. This was also a short-lived initiative. As was easy to predict, the subtleties of the party's role in the cabinet were irrelevant to the public and the political costs to the Christian Democrats became unbearable. It soon found an excuse to force their two ministers out of the government. Pérez reacted by switching the minister of defense to the Ministry of Foreign Affairs and replacing him with a general that had a less tolerant attitude towards rebel army officers.

This failure to form a more broadly based cabinet gave further confirmation of Pérez's political weakness, and it gave greater ammunition to his opponents. Calls for the president's resignation multiplied, as did demands for the dismissal of Congress and the election of a temporary group charged with reforming the Constitution. Protesters demanded the restructuring of the Supreme Court, replacement of its current members (the appointees of *Acción Democrática* or the Christian Democrats) with independent judges, and an overhaul of the corrupt, inefficient judicial system. As the atmosphere became even more charged, Pérez made additional adjustments. While not backtracking on any of the economic reforms, he froze the plan to gradually increase the price of gasoline and postponed increasing electricity rates for several months. The president reshuffled his cabinet again and made other institutional changes. None of these measures, however, was of any major consequence in reducing the political unrest.

Calls for Pérez's resignation intensified in the subsequent months. It became evident, however, that Pérez intended to stay. He flatly refused to even consider the possibility of stepping down before his term in office was over. His firmness introduced a small element of predictability in an environment filled with uncertainty. But it also spurred into action those who wanted Pérez out at any cost or who saw in his ouster an opportunity to further their own political ambitions.

While public demonstrations and protests occurred more frequently, they were mostly concentrated among radical student groups who took advantage of the government's inability to contain their street actions. The government continued to seek some form of alliance with other political forces, but with little success. Various groups of businessmen, civic leaders, and others attempted to create a platform for a broad-based national alliance, also without success. An initiative to hold a national referendum on shortening Pérez's presidential term was approved by Congress only to be overturned on constitutional grounds by the Supreme Court.

Pérez waited patiently for the political turbulence to die down. With state and local elections scheduled for the end of 1992 and presidential elections for December 1993, general confusion and disarray among the main political actors, and without strong leadership or a coherent political strategy, the advantages of lying low and waiting out his term became obvious. While pointed criticism of the president and the government went unabated, at the time no individual or political group seemed sufficiently powerful to do more than block the initiatives of others. While this stalemate made it very difficult for the Pérez administration to maintain the rapid pace its reform program had attained in its first three years, it also made it equally impossible for groups opposing the reforms to bring about any major reversals.

Instability nevertheless took its toll. International enthusiasm to invest in Venezuela (at an all-time high just before the coup) decreased sharply; gaining congressional support for tax laws necessary to fend off drastic fiscal deterioration became enormously difficult; and turnover among government technocrats further weakened the government's capacity to design and execute public policy.

Here We Go Again: Another Coup

> The motivation of our insurrection was to reclaim democracy and our unfaltering decision is to eradicate corruption in a nation of obscene privileges and nightmarish poverty. Government corruption has abolished all notion of ethics in the handling of public monies. We will stop this chaotic state of affairs.[43]

Thus spoke air force General Francisco Visconti from Peru, where he and ninety-two other Venezuelan officers and soldiers sought and received political asylum after their failed attempt to overthrow the government. General Visconti, two rear admirals, one army colonel, and one lieutenant colonel from the national guard led an uprising the night of November 27, 1992. In charge of supplies and logistics in the Ministry of Defense, Visconti and Rear Admirals Gruber and Cabrera were members of the Joint Chiefs of Staff. The previous military revolt was undertaken by mid-ranking and junior officers in the army. Instead, the November coup was led by high-ranking officers in the navy and the air force, and the units that participated were essentially from the air force. Civilian participation in the planning and undertaking of the first uprising was limited to members of the radical leftist fringe, whereas in the second coup attempt, a broader, and heterogeneous coalition of civilian groups was involved.[44]

The rebels went into action at dawn by taking over the state television station. They also captured the main antennas in the mountains over Caracas, effectively controlling the signals of all but one commercial television channel. They seized control of two strategic air bases and initiated bombing raids over the presidential palace and other military and security installations.

After taking over the television station, the rebels began broadcasting a four-minute video that Lieutenant Colonel Chávez had secretly taped in prison. Appearing in front of the Venezuelan flag in his uniform and red beret and projecting the folk-hero image he had gained following the February uprising, he called on Venezuelans to take to the streets and topple the government. This, he said, was the only way of "ending tyranny and starting a new era of true democracy." Chávez's message was broadcast several times in the few hours that the rebels controlled the channel. A group of them wearing civilian clothes and gripping their guns menacingly appeared several times live and called for the poor to come down from the barrios with "bottles, sticks, or any other weapon at hand" to seek justice and launch a people's revolution.

Another videotape with a message from the leaders of the uprising was never broadcast by the rebels. In it, the four high-ranking officers (dressed in their full military regalia) who were responsible for staging the coup delivered a different message. They said that many diverse social groups made up their movement which they called "July 5" (the date of the Venezuelan declaration of independence). After recounting the many economic and moral ills afflicting Venezuelan society and stressing the need to oust Pérez, they asserted that the military and civilian forces they commanded had strict orders to treat all prisoners respectfully and humanely, including Pérez, and that measures would be taken to prevent acts of violence against individuals and private property. Peace throughout the country would be rapidly restored, and all international treaties and agreements entered into by the state would be maintained. A government of national consensus would be established until free democratic elections could be called.[45] Broadcasting this message might have induced a much more positive reaction among the population than had the sight of the aggressive and intimidating armed civilians.

What had happened was that the group within the military that organized this second coup was different from the one that led the February uprising. While both sought to overthrow the government, their composition, aims, methods, and civil alliances were very different, giving rise to deep rivalries and tensions among them. Once it became evident that the high-ranking officers were going to go ahead with a coup before the local and state elections scheduled for December 6, the other group was forced to join them. But in what was called "a coup within the coup," a few armed civilians in the Chávez faction took advantage of the situation, got to the television station first, and aired only the Chávez videotape. This gave the impression that the uprising was a second attempt by the same group, while in fact this coup was being staged by a rival group within the armed forces.[46]

Once again, the coup failed and the government regained control of the situation in less than a day. While the rebels were able to launch continuous air raids against critical sites in Caracas, they lacked the ground forces needed to take control of them. Even their air attacks were somewhat ineffectual, given that, whether due to sheer incompetence or the deliberate sabotage of ground crews, many of the bombs they dropped failed to explode. Expensive and sophisticated Mirage jet fighters flew over the capital throughout the morning, terrorizing the population. They were unable to fire a single shot, however, because as was later disclosed, their weapons systems were not operational. In a last-ditch attempt, General Visconti jumped into a Mirage and flew over the city several times, breaking the sound barrier and shattering the glass windows in many Caracas homes, along with the nerves of much of the population.

Visconti then returned to the air force base in Maracay and, before army units loyal to the government were able to attack, he took off in a C-130 transport plane along with the rest of the insurgents and flew to Peru. Chávez never left his prison cell, and his armed civilian allies in the radical leftist groups, *Bandera Roja* (Red Flag) and *Tercer Camino* (Third Road), who had taken part in some of the street actions in Caracas, retreated very early in the morning after their calls for the population to take to the streets went unheard.

In theory, the televised messages were supposed to spark a massive popular uprising which, in turn, would lead the rest of the armed forces to join in the coup against Pérez. Instead, out of cynicism towards politics or basic self-preservation, people stayed at home. Once again, the coup was poorly coordinated and was not supported by other civilian or military groups of any significance.

Given the political atmosphere that preceded the coup, it was easy to overestimate the social and political support that such a move would have. Continuous and extremely aggressive political attacks against Pérez were amply disseminated by the media and, in some cases, even initiated by them. Widespread popular discontent created by the harsh economic conditions was exacerbated by bitter criticism of Pérez by such highly respected national figures as the writer, Arturo Uslar Pietri, who repeatedly called for his resignation. Internally, the armed forces were deeply divided, and it was not uncommon for high ranking officers to voice their great dissatisfaction with the government openly.

The leaders of the coup failed to translate this atmosphere of intense discontent and criticism into effective action in support of their initiative. Many potential military supporters of the coup held off until the chances of the revolt succeeding became clearer. Others were put off by the sight of Chávez and the armed civilians on television. Many, it later turned out, had never really been prepared to go beyond recriminations.

In addition, in the wake of the first coup, the government greatly strengthened the surveillance of officers and others who could potentially take part in an uprising. While government intelligence failed yet again to prevent the coup, this time it was better prepared to minimize the scope of the rebels' actions. Government security services were able to head off additional units that were ready to join the rebels. As a result, all the action related to the uprising was concentrated in Caracas and the air base in Maracay, and the rebels met with defeat.

The government regained the support of most political parties, labor, and the private sector. Their leaders immediately abandoned their bellicose stance toward the government and made television appearances to denounce the coup and call for the preservation of democracy. By the time normalcy was restored, more than five hundred officers and a large contingent of soldiers had been arrested or had fled to Peru. More than two hundred people died (most in a jail riot sparked by inmates taking advantage of the uprising to escape). The sites that had been bombarded sustained serious damage, and several planes were lost.

After the Second Coup Attempt: Ballots Not Bullets

While this second attempted overthrow did little to restore the people's sympathy for Pérez, it did generate considerable popular resentment against the military rebels. Watching in terror as military planes bombarded their targets in the middle of densely populated areas or as jet fighters flew at low altitudes and caused repeated sonic booms, the population had good reason to fear the military. Chávez's image as a patriotic or heroic figure was damaged by his television appearance and those of his supporters. For the first time, the possibility of a violent and incompetent military dictatorship acquired a more concrete meaning for the many citizens who had thought that an honest and benevolent military government might be a realistic hope for the future.

Local elections were another factor that helped diminish support for any violent actions against the government. Political cynicism and a deep-seated distrust of politicians and the political system were rampant in Venezuela. One aspect of the political process that still retained some legitimacy among the population was the direct election of state governors, city mayors, and other local officials. These elections were held for the first time in December 1989 and were scheduled again for December 1992.

The military officers who planned the second coup knew that they had to stage it prior to these elections. Participation in the electoral process would not diminish the popular rejection of the government, but it would create more stakeholders in the current democratic regime. Newly elected officials would be more interested in letting Pérez complete his last year in office and avoid contributing to instabilities that might jeopardize their own positions. State governors and other local officials had loyal and active followings they could mobilize, making a military uprising much more risky.

Nine days after the failed coup, Venezuelans went to the polls to elect 22 state governors, 282 city mayors, 2,116 members of city councils and approximately 3,000 members of parish boards, a newly created political body operating at a level below that of the city council. Voters could choose from more than 600 officially recognized national or local political groups that endorsed candidates for the different offices.

Voter turnout was higher than for the 1989 elections and much higher than what surveys held prior to the coup attempt had anticipated. Opposition parties, especially the Christian Democrats and *La Causa R* increased their share of the vote and posted significant advances over *Acción Democrática*, even though it retained a significant number of offices. But the most important outcome of the elections by far was the exercise of individual electoral judgment: voters based their selections on the candidates' characters and, in the case of incumbent governors, on their performances rather than on the leanings of the party bosses. Only a few years earlier, the party hierarchy had had complete control over appointments to these public offices. In the elections of 1992, the winning candidates had much greater popular support than their political parties.

In contrast to what the media and most analysts had claimed, the candidates' positions vis-à-vis Pérez's economic reforms did not affect their electoral chances. One illustration of the complexity of the political situation is given by the two governors who won by the largest landslides (Osvaldo Alvarez Paz in the state of Zulia and Enrique Salas Romer in the state of Carabobo). Both were from the Christian Democratic party and were also staunch supporters of the government's economic program! By contrast, in a surprise upset, the incumbent mayor of Caracas, Claudio Fermin, a critic of the economic reforms, a rising star of the government party, and a protege of President Pérez, lost that important race. (He was later nominated by *Acción Democrática* as its presidential candidate for the 1993 elections.)

The elections did not dispel the possibility of another coup, much less create a stable political and social environment. Even with elections to choose Pérez's successor scheduled for the end of 1993, calls for his resignation or ouster continued, along with bitter criticism of his economic policies and constant accusations of corruption that eventually forced him from power in May of 1993.

Chapter 7
Some Explanations

Chile and Mexico began the transition toward economies less centered around the state earlier than most other Latin American countries. In the rest of the region economic reforms began after the mid-1980s, and by the early 1990s all the Latin American countries were in the throes of the process of liberalizing trade, privatizing state-owned enterprises, deregulating entire sectors of the economy, fighting fiscal deficits, and hoping that their private sectors could compete in world markets. The pace and scope of reforms varied from country to country, but in all of them, the direction of the changes was the same—more market and less state.

Venezuela seemed to be well positioned to undertake this transition, thus the extraordinarily traumatic reactions and consequences caught the government and most observers by surprise. After all, Argentina under Carlo Menem, Colombia under Cesar Gaviria, and several countries in Central America had pursued roughly similar reforms without incurring such enormous political costs as beset Venezuela's government. Many of the same destabilizing forces that surfaced in Venezuela are bound to have been present in these other countries as well. It seems however that they were either neutralized by other conditions, that they lacked the same intensity, or that they are still brewing under the surface and will eventually become more apparent. It may also well be the case that hyperinflation, military dictatorships, and wars had inoculated these countries' populations with a dose of tolerance for the immediate effects of the reforms which Venezuelans, having been spared these experiences, lacked. A comparative analysis of the reasons why political instability surged with such intensity in Venezuela and not in other countries is beyond the scope of this book. This analysis centers instead on the many factors that converged to generate the inflammable social and political atmosphere that threatened South America's longest continuous democracy.

Understanding the circumstances that brought about Venezuela's political turmoil sheds light on the political challenges of managing large-scale economic change. This turmoil was the product of several forces acting simultaneously. Internal problems and deep divisions within the armed forces, the political effects of inevitable but highly unpopular economic reforms, the role of the media in amplifying instability, the private sector's resistance to the process, and the mistakes made by the government were significant contributing factors. But an even more basic cause of the nation's political instability was the institutional devastation of the state. The profound deterioration of all public institutions had rendered the state incapable of responding adequately to the many demands of the moment. This, in turn, was a reflection of the deep crisis that political parties, labor unions, business associations, political institutions, and even cultural and intellectual groups had been experiencing for many years. The nature and depth of this generalized crisis became more evident as the stress of coping with so many unprecedented challenges took its toll and the weakness of these institutions could no longer be hidden.

The Military: The Consequences of a Truncated Pyramid

The situation within the armed forces was a logical extension of prevailing conditions within the country, the state, and the economy. Certain longstanding trends had eaten away at the function and the ethos of the Venezuelan armed forces. First, for many years, the rigor of the promotion system had been gradually relaxed. This permitted the number of senior officers to increase at a much faster pace than the number of positions available. This trend accelerated in the 1980s and systematically undermined the hierarchical pyramid on which military organization relies. In effect, each year, more and more generals occupied posts that just a few years earlier had customarily been assigned to captains. Too many generals and admirals were chasing too few real jobs within the armed forces, putting the promotion system under great strain. Individual merit very quickly ceased to be the overriding condition for promotion and career advancement. The need to have friends and mentors within and without the armed forces became as important as having the necessary qualifications. This stimulated strong rivalries between individuals and the small informal groups or "clans" to which they belonged. Therefore, significant pressure existed for aspiring officers, their mentors, and proteges to block or even sabotage the career advances of their rivals.[47]

Adding to the comparative weight of factors unrelated to individual merit was a law mandating congressional approval for all promotions to the rank of colonel and general. Although originally envisioned as a healthy check by civil society on the military, the law became an instrument of politicization, barely concealed partisanship, and an incentive for the discrediting tactics that rival officers and their clans commonly employed against each other.

Under these circumstances, the interservice rivalries that in all armed forces shape military organizational behavior acquired a far more divisive role. And not only did competition for budgets, resources, and career opportunities develop among the army, the navy, and the air force, it mushroomed within each branch as well. Competition was intensified by the fiscal crises of the 1980s, when military budgets were tightened and foreign exchange for arms procurement and maintenance became harder to secure. Moreover, between 1980 and 1988, the number of military personnel nearly doubled (from forty-one thousand to seventy-one thousand men) as the economy worsened and the military offered one of the few employment options for many poor Venezuelans. Also as a consequence of the fiscal crisis, the portion of the military budget allocated to foreign exchange grew increasingly larger as the daily needs of soldiers and junior officers went unmet. While major outlays were made to purchase U.S. F-16 fighter planes, sophisticated French tanks, and Italian warships, soldiers had to get by with insufficient supplies of boots, uniforms, housing, and other basics. Officers' salaries declined to such a degree that they could no longer afford cars or even adequate housing. In 1991, the monthly net salary of a lieutenant was the equivalent of U.S. $200. It became common for several junior officers and their families to share a single apartment in poor barrios. This created resentment toward senior officers, who were increasingly isolated from their subordinates and interested almost exclusively in the economics of procurement and the politics of promotion.

The lack of cohesion between junior officers and their superiors was also exacerbated by generational differences: while junior officers had had ample opportunities to complement their military education with professional studies at home and abroad, this was not the case for older officers. These were part of the cohort of officers whose academic training in the mid-1960s had been cut short by troop call-ups for the war against the leftist guerrillas. All this contributed greatly to the tension and mistrust between senior officers and their subordinates, adding to erosion of discipline and organizational fragmentation.

Finally, two traits common to all public-sector organizations in Venezuela also affected the armed forces: rapid turnover and lack of clear, stable organizational goals. The average tenure of the minister of defense (who has always been a senior military officer) has been one year. When that year is up, the minister normally reaches retirement age and has to step down both from government and from active military duty. Such regular turnover is one source of instability, politicking, and inefficiency within the armed forces, and it greatly hampers sustained efforts at institutional and organizational development. A second source of instability is the rapidly changing domestic and international conditions. These have caused a great deal of confusion regarding the precise role of the armed forces in a country with the geopolitical, social, and economic characteristics of Venezuela. This confusion has kept any unified and shared vision from emerging, an essential component of maintaining a common sense of direction within a complex organization. As an end result of these trends within the armed forces, central authority and control became increasingly difficult to maintain.

The Economy: Record Growth Does Not Political Stability Buy

As outlined in chapter 5, the Venezuelan economy reacted very fast and very favorably to the adjustments of 1989. In 1990 it entered a high-growth phase that appeared at least temporarily to be immune to the profound political shocks that later shattered investor confidence in the country. Just prior to the first coup attempt, Venezuela's 10 percent GDP growth made it the world's fastest growing economy in the world. It surpassed the performance of economic powerhouses like Singapore (6.5 percent), Malaysia (8.6 percent), Thailand (7.9 percent), and Indonesia (7 percent). Its expansion of output far exceeded the major industrial countries' average (2 percent) and Latin America's as a whole (2.6 percent).[48] In the private sector 430,000 new jobs were created—the largest increase in more than a decade. This boosted private-sector formal employment to 4.2 million workers, a new high. Moreover, informal employment diminished for the first time in eight years (by 130,000 persons), and unemployment decreased by 85,000 persons, lowering the unemployment rate from almost 10 percent the previous year to 8.5 percent. The current account of the balance of payments in 1991 showed a surplus of about $8 billion; international reserves reached $14 billion; and the stock of foreign investment advanced to its highest level since the mid-1970s. The fiscal deficit was less than 3 percent of GNP, the exchange rate remained stable, and the stock market enjoyed a second boom year.[49]

The year 1991 was a good one not only in terms of macroeconomic aggregates. It was also a year in which the unit volume of domestic consumption of poultry increased by 41 percent, rice by 30 percent, pasta (a staple among low-income groups) by 25 percent, and sugar by 20 percent. Overall the food-processing industry expanded by 11 percent in volume. Furthermore, the apparel market grew by 28 percent (excluding imports), the number of cars sold increased by 72 percent over the previous year, and the household appliance sector had its best season ever.[50] As figures 23 and 24 illustrate, in 1991 the sales volumes of consumer goods in general and of food products in particular reached their highest levels in more than a decade.

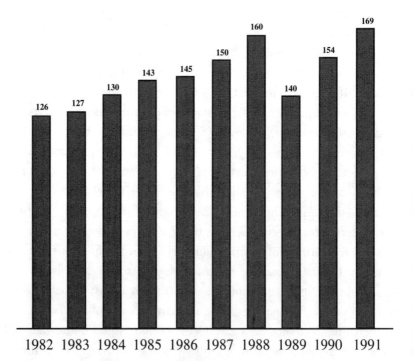

1982 1983 1984 1985 1986 1987 1988 1989 1990 1991

In volume, base year 1976 = 100.

Figure 23. The Market for Consumer Products
Source: DATOS, 1991.

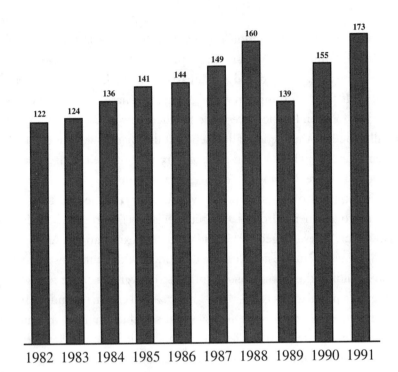

1982 1983 1984 1985 1986 1987 1988 1989 1990 1991

In volume, base year 1976 = 100.

Figure 24. The Market for Food Products
Source: DATOS, 1991.

These record-setting numbers created great enthusiasm among businessmen, government officials, and foreign investors. This was not the case however among local politicians, journalists, and the majority of the population. By and large, they remained unimpressed by the statistics and highly critical of the government's economic policies. Often, the government's critics were the cast-offs of the previous system—the individuals and groups that had lost privileges and power under the new scheme. But there were other disinterested observers who also expressed serious misgivings, not to mention, of course, the general dissatisfaction among the population. Inflation had become firmly lodged at 30 percent annually and continued to eat away at the poor and middle classes' buying power, remaining a foremost source of social friction. While in 1991 real salaries increased for the first time in many years, they still lagged behind the needs and expectations created by decades of an artificially maintained economy. Also, while food consumption was growing, the share of family budgets going to food and basic necessities reached new highs—bringing to an all-time low the income allotment families had to devote to other expenditures which had been a customary part of their consumption patterns. (Figure 25 shows net per capita income.)

Frustration over rising prices was further amplified by the slow pace of government efforts to target special social programs directly to the poor. These lagged far behind needs and expectations. Although massive, inefficient subsidies can be done away with almost instantaneously, building the institutions required to deliver assistance to highly vulnerable populations takes much longer. As all countries undergoing major structural reforms are discovering, social safety nets are much easier to design than to implement. Other basic state-run services—health, housing, education, and urban transportation—had also been drastically curtailed by a decade of fiscal crises and mismanagement. The economic adjustment process and ineffective or delayed government actions made this situation worse. The condition of public services was a constant source of anger toward the government, and those affected tended to dismiss any claims of macroeconomic advances. Hospitals that fail to function; an unreliable and insufficient water supply system; a bus system incapable of bringing urban workers back and forth to their jobs; a school system in a shambles—these realities devastated government popularity. Additionally, unprecedented levels of street crime and the government's apparent failure to handle the personal safety crisis provoked a strong outcry against the administration from all quarters.

News of a solid balance of payments or of world record-setting levels of economic growth did little to mollify the negative attitudes born of such tangible public problems. The widely held perception that no explicit effort was being made to rectify the profoundly inequitable

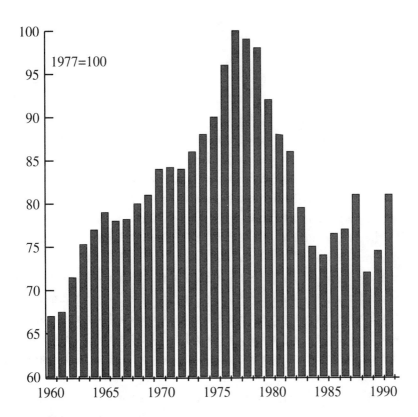

Figure 25. Per Capita Income
Source: Kelly, 1992.

distribution of income and wealth that years of demagogic and ill-conceived government intervention had spawned served to reinforce these attitudes. Fortunes were being made in the soaring stock market, previously banned luxury imports filled shopping malls, and those privileged few with savings safely and profitably deposited in foreign banks flaunted their wealth with a newfound market-ethos. The great majority of the population thus became convinced that reforms unduly benefited a small group of businessmen, speculators, and politicians at the expense of society at large. Aggravating this sense of inequity was the enormous wealth that a small elite had been allowed to accumulate under the previous policies. The Venezuelan rich tend to be as ostentatious as their counterparts everywhere and provided daily proof that economic reforms did not affect their living standards. That the burden of paying for the mistakes of the past was not being shared equally by everyone became all too apparent.

The government repeatedly insisted that the hardships imposed by the new economic policies were unavoidable. It also contended that the social costs of its reforms were much lower than those that would ensue if corrections were not implemented—that is, hyperinflation and its ravaging consequences. The government correctly argued that any attempt at forcing the rich to bring back the fortunes they kept well hidden abroad was bound to fail and that it would only hamper the voluntary repatriation that was beginning to take place, spurred by new investment opportunities.

While these may be valid points, they are based in counterfactual arguments that rely on hypothetical possibilities to which most Venezuelans could relate neither intellectually nor through their personal history. The country had never experienced anything like the circumstances it was going through, far less the ordeals of hyperinflation. The day-to-day hardships and frustrations were neither remote nor hypothetical; they were perceived as the direct consequences of government actions. The economic malaise—which public opinion attributed to politicians in general and to the Pérez government in particular—contributed to a social and political ferment that exacerbated the instability prompted by the aborted coups.

Nevertheless, it would be misguided to conclude that the state of the economy was the fundamental force underlying the Venezuelan political and institutional crisis. Rather, the economy was rapidly recovering and serious macroeconomic imbalances were being cured;

but far more had been expected, since the economic program replaced the all-encompassing, state-centered approach that had held sway for decades. In effect, the economic stabilization program had to fulfill political and ideological functions for which it was neither designed nor suited.[51] Furthermore, in the eyes of public opinion, the new economic policies were the cause of the operational collapse of public services and social service delivery agencies, though these had been neglected or exploited for years.

At the same time, while the economic crisis was far from over, the economy was rapidly becoming an instrument of political stability, as small but influential social groups gradually started to support the new market-oriented approach, and results were becoming more apparent. But while the economy tended to stabilize, the social and political systems exhibited a disarray that overwhelmed all else and eventually came to affect the economy as well.

The Political Economy of Corruption

After each of the two failed coups, most politicians blamed the economic policies and stressed the need to reverse them. But the coups also mobilized individuals and groups who were newcomers to the political debate, and politicians soon found themselves on the defensive. Criticism of the behavior and role of political parties, corruption, and the administration of justice dominated public opinion and the general mood of the country. The magnitude of the political and institutional crisis reflected not only the standoff between a government imposing unpopular changes and political groups opposing them and jockeying for position. Forces deeply ingrained in the moral, social, and political fabric of the country were at work as well.

Corruption became the lightning rod that attracted the anger and frustrations of all segments of society. It had existed and flourished ever since oil wealth had endowed the state with massive resources to distribute with little oversight or accountability to taxpayers. But during the second Pérez administration it acquired an unprecedented political significance.

Government corruption mainly originates in three kinds of activities: the sale of public assets, the procurement of goods and services, and the state's intervention in the economy. The more the state intervenes, the greater the opportunities for profitable collusion between government officials and those who can benefit from biased public decisions. Transactions in which the government is either the seller (as in all privatizations) or the buyer (as in all procurement activities) are susceptible to influence from bribes and kickbacks. From Italy to Japan and from the United States to the People's Republic of China, when the state sells a public asset or when money is exchanged for highways, guns, food for public hospitals, or supplies for public schools, opportunities for corruption arise.

From this perspective and in contrast to the dominant perception, corruption must have greatly diminished during the Pérez government in comparison to what it had been in the past. This is principally because in eliminating most government controls (on prices, on the exchange rate, on interest rates, on imports and exports, on credits, and so forth) the possibilities for government officials to weight decisions in favor of a specific individual or firm were greatly diminished. Furthermore, all the major decisions related to privatization (even the hiring of consultants and financial advisers) were arrived at through open international auctions accessible to all interested parties. Also, the Pérez administration had to operate under an unprecedentedly vigorous degree of scrutiny from the media and most organized groups of society. This scrutiny is bound to have had some impact on curbing the excesses of the public sector, which had an enormous propensity for corruption bred by many years of opportunity and impunity. This state of affairs had resulted from the lack of effective controls, the practical nonexistence of an honest judicial system, and from the mass media which, under the old economic regime, had been much more tolerant given their own dependency on the government's goodwill for their profitability.

The traditional tolerance for corruption which the general public had exhibited for decades practically disappeared. It mattered little to the public that the potential for corruption had been undermined by the new policies. Why then was corruption the source of such widespread dissatisfaction and violent opposition to the government? There are at least four reasons for this paradox.

First, the bulk of the population harbored two deeply ingrained beliefs: that Venezuela was a very rich country and that it was impoverished by the corruption and thievery of the rich and powerful. Instead of blaming macroeconomic mismanagement, sharply reduced oil revenues, or incompetence, people blamed the country's economic crisis on corruption. With the unprecedented daily economic tribulations, the concept of corruption took on a concrete and personal meaning as opposed to the abstract problem of political ethics and economic power it had been in the past. Second, while the government denounced the corruption that pervaded the economic schemes it was dismantling, it did little to bring those suspected of unethical practices to justice. This fueled the perception that the government was soft to the point of complicity.

Third, while the president appointed to his cabinet a group of relatively young and politically independent technocrats who were generally perceived as honest and competent, he also appointed individuals to head some crucial agencies whose unsavory reputations or poor performance hampered the administration's credibility and tarnished its public image. Fourth, the media echoed the frustrations of the population and heightened them, becoming more active and audacious than ever in disclosing and denouncing corruption, bringing it to the forefront of any discussion of government and public policy. This vigilance and outspokenness stood in sharp contrast to the verdicts of the courts; in almost all cases, those accused were found innocent or were able to flee the country. Corruption and its economic and political consequences created the classic scenario where anger and hunger combine to create an inflammable political and social mixture. As a side-effect, the passivity with which Venezuelans had previously viewed this illicit behavior all but disappeared. Unfortunately, their unexpected demands for justice and punishment of those involved in scandals could not be satisfied by a judicial system that was itself paralyzed by corruption and incompetence.

The Conglomerates Go to War

That entrenched private conglomerates would fight any government attempt forcing greater competition on them was to be expected. In fact, deregulating the economy and eliminating government rules that stifled competition became yet another source of opposition to the Pérez government. An effect which no one anticipated however, and which proved far more destabilizing than business groups' resistance to the reforms, was the warfare that broke out among such economic groups. The competition induced by reforms spurred these large conglomerates into an all-out war with one another for control of the newly created opportunities in the economy. An already besieged government found itself in the middle of these battles. In accordance with the longstanding practice of big business in developing countries, these battles were fought more in the political arena than in the marketplace.

In a state-centered economy, many years of pervasive government intervention create market structures in which competition is dormant and oligopolistic behavior prevalent. Collusion and tactics to exclude actual or potential rivals become the core of firms' business strategies. Eventually a precarious equilibrium between the existing corporations is reached whereby each group avoids intruding in the others' activities. The balance is periodically upset and ruinous battles ensue. Government decisions or other factors may alter business conditions in a given sector, triggering a series of moves and countermoves from the dominant groups in the sector.

In Venezuela, surviving the threats of a constantly changing policy environment and the predatory moves of rivals was difficult without having access to politicians and policymakers and the means to influence them. Maintaining close ties with union leaders who could oppose or promote a specific government decision in the name of the working class became a frequently utilized tactic. Another was to employ journalists as highly paid consultants to write or broadcast targeted news items about competitors or influence government decisions through the media. In fact, during the first years of the Pérez administration the longstanding tendency of industrial and financial conglomerates diversifying their holdings to include media companies intensified greatly. Banks and other financial firms bought newspapers and radio stations, paying sums that could never be justified by the profits these businesses could ever turn on their own.

Gains in productivity obtained by many years of hard work or significant investments could be completely wiped out by the connivance of a public regulator and a rival. It was, therefore, not uncommon for large private companies to develop intelligence gathering capacities, sometime hiring retired or even active police officers and intelligence professionals. After all, a tape containing the private telephone conversation of a rival or a government official could be infinitely more profitable than the design specifications of a new product.

When market-oriented reforms and deregulation increased domestic and foreign competition, the arrangements, pacts, and other agreements among conglomerates broke down, and the equilibrium they had reached was upturned. In certain cases, this pushed some of these large conglomerates into a competitive frenzy in which they used every weapon at their disposal, including government officials, politicians, journalists, union leaders, and intelligence gatherers, to try to ruin their rivals or to gain a dominant position in a given industry.

The deregulation of the financial sector and of the stock market, the privatization of large public utilities or state-owned manufacturing enterprises, the takeover of existing firms in alliance with foreign investors, and countless other opportunities opened the door for new competition among business groups. While their politically based tactical weapons may lose their effectiveness in the long run and may even come to be abandoned, they have continued to play a major role as tools to support the conglomerates' business strategies during the transition. The added complexity, disinformation, and instability such behavior injected into an already turbulent and confusing political environment was considerable.

In many instances the government found itself in the middle of these wars. Typically, each side would exert great pressures to get the government to act in its behalf. When the government did not, articles, editorials, and even purported news items appeared in the media, showing how the government had been bought by one or the other of the groups in the dispute. This pattern added to the perception of generalized corruption.

Illusory Institutions:
The Weakness of the State and the Parties

No single factor contributed as much to the political instability following the attempted coups as the weakness of the state. The Venezuelan state has often been accused of being too rich by virtue of its oil revenues, too large on account of its ownership of an array of firms, or too powerful because of its role in most aspects of economic and social life. Paradoxically, however, having all these attributes enormously weakened the state, minimizing the reliability of its institutions and its capacity to perform its basic functions with a modicum of efficiency.

The demands on the state have been propelled not only by population growth and rising expectations. The policy approach that prevailed for three decades continuously expanded the scope of state action. As the public sector was burdened with added functions and responsibilities, the deterioration of its performance accelerated. The chronic fiscal crises made it impossible to sustain the appropriate funding levels required for the expanded public functions. An underpaid and poorly trained civil service plagued by turnover, corruption, congestion, and politicization severely eroded the capacity of public agencies to do their jobs.

But the state was not only weakened by the number of policies it had to formulate, implement, finance, and monitor. It was also weakened by the approach it took in defining the nature of these policies. With few exceptions, each new policy initiative required a public bureaucracy to implement it, and this normally implied an inordinate amount of discretion on the part of civil servants. This bureaucratic approach created fertile conditions for corruption to take hold. It also paid off handsomely those particular interest groups who centered their efforts on forcing or persuading bureaucrats and politicians to make decisions and grant concessions in their favor. This again diminished the state's autonomy, further eroding its function.

It followed logically that, over time, the state became ever more focused on responding to the pressures, needs, and requests of influential groups and individuals. This decreased its capacity to implement policies and make decisions aimed at serving the population as a whole. The state and in particular the executive branch came to depend for their survival on the political support of those specific groups that benefited from their policies. Dependence on narrow segments of society inhibited the development of mechanisms that might have enabled the state to build the broad political support needed to win approval of policies benefiting the general public at the expense of small but well organized special interests. This is a common pattern in most democracies, but in Venezuela the low level of social organization and the capture of the main parties—and thereby the government—by these special interests blotted out any possibility of adopting policies these small privileged groups opposed for a very long time.

Ironically, by choosing an economic policy aimed at transferring to the market important decisions that had been the traditional province of government officials, a very weak state deliberately made itself weaker. All at once, the power that had accompanied the capacity to allocate foreign exchange, set prices, import or bar a specific product, assign or withhold a social subsidy was surrendered. The government suddenly had nothing to give the influential groups and individuals who had supported all recent administrations in exchange for privileged access to special favors. Most notable among these influential groups whose favor the government lost was its own party, *Acción Democrática*.

Like all Venezuelan political parties, in recent years *Acción Democrática* had come to rely almost exclusively on its ability to act as a broker in the distribution of the state's favors. The government's surprising decision to reduce its own discretion in economic matters left the party with very little to offer to its members, given that ideology or any other moral stance had long since ceased to be important as a source of partisan commitment.

This problem was not limited to *Acción Democrática*. All political parties and special interests—including those representing labor, business, and professionals—were left reeling after having depended for too long on the special concessions they exacted from the state to justify their existence to their constituents. Furthermore, within all parties and interest groups a significant rift emerged between those who continued to be committed to the more statist and nationalistic model of import substitution and the small but growing faction that favored a more market- and export-oriented approach.

These internal divisions, the profound ideological confusion brought on by changes within and without the country, and the political parties' crumbling foundations and organizational abilities ravaged what remained of the parties' internal cohesion. These conditions also limited their capacity to define and sustain a coherent political strategy, restricting their effectiveness as political actors. These weaknesses helped facilitate the introduction of reforms by circumscribing the effectiveness of the opposition. But the institutional weakness of most of Venezuela's social and political actors later proved to be a major obstacle to regaining the political stability that the country had enjoyed for many years.

The Media Barons Take Over

The mass media proved to be another destabilizing factor spawned by the government's abdication of power over economic decisions. Like most other private firms, the newspapers, television, and radio networks were usually owned by diversified conglomerates with business interests in different sectors. As such, they had been critically dependent on government decisions under the previous economic scheme.

Freedom of expression had long been a central tenet of democratic political life in Venezuela, and every government had been extremely sensitive to criticisms in this domain. In general, both the print and electronic media demonstrated a somewhat adversarial attitude toward the government. Nonetheless, easily discernible limits beyond which owners and editors never ventured to criticize government gave evidence of a tacit understanding. This implicit inhibition was abandoned with economic reforms, and the mass media acquired an unprecedented vehemence in their attacks against the government, reporting and amplifying with a vengeance their strident opposition to it. Several forces pushed the media to adopt this belligerent stance.

First, the mood of the country was without a doubt one of anger toward government policies and the impunity of corrupt individuals. The media had not created these deeply negative attitudes. This was a social reality that became a basic element of any domestic news coverage. But the demand for scapegoats was high, and in the atmosphere of intensified competition the media, like other businesses, competed fiercely to satisfy their readers, viewers, and listeners.

A second factor was the typical propensity of the mass media in democratic societies to develop adversarial relationships with those in power. Third, media conglomerates also engaged in oligopolistic warfare with all its ensuing consequences. Fourth, some media owners continued to press the government for special concessions. If the government acquiesced, the rival oligopolies would retaliate against it through the media they controlled. If the government denied a concession, the spurned party took aim. In all cases, some aspect of the government—not necessarily related to the specific demand—was severely criticized.

Fifth, for a variety of reasons, journalists tended to strongly oppose the economic reform program. Their training made them suspicious and distrustful of the market, and as a group, they belonged to a socioeconomic stratum—lower middle-class professionals—that was hard hit by inflation and declining living standards. As a profession, they also suffered from the countrywide neglect of economic education, making it difficult for them to understand, and no less report, the nature, purposes, and consequences of the government's economic actions. Government spokespersons shared similar limitations, restricting the development of an effective information strategy that might at least have partially offset the effect of journalists' and media owners' opposition.

The government systematically failed to recognize that under these circumstances, an effective communication strategy had to be one of its top priorities. Instead, a decimated government continued to handle public information with the same assumptions, institutions, and attitudes it had inherited. It ignored the reality that it had cut itself off from the instruments on which previous governments usually relied to keep media owners and journalists from holding it hostage to their interests. In the past, the possibility of using the subtle but powerful influence arising from its many economic decisions allowed the government to neglect the development of a reliable capacity to inform the public and explain its decisions. Such an institutional capacity would not have prevented the political turmoil that emerged. But it would have been a dramatic improvement over the image of a mute, unexplaining government trying to bring about fundamental societal change.

All of these factors boosted the power of media owners and editors to unprecedented levels. Internally divided political parties, ineffectual business associations and labor unions, an incompetent and corrupt judiciary, an embattled government, and dilapidated social institutions created a vacuum of power that was filled by the media. The influence of media groups was limited only by the actions of their rivals. But, in fact, during the Pérez administration no other institution held more sway over the country's situation than the media, and no groups were more powerful than those that controlled them.

New Economics and Old Politics: The Government's Big Mistake

President Pérez embraced a new set of assumptions and ideas about the management of the economy. But, in what later proved to be a crucial mistake, he continued to operate with most of the assumptions that had been used to guide political actions and tactics in Venezuela in the past. Such an approach proved to be as inadequate for dealing with the political situation as the old interventionist schemes had been for dealing with the country's economic crisis. The lack of consistency between the economic and political strategies of the Pérez government became a major source of social turmoil and political instability.

The old political approaches were effective when the state had many economic levers to which it could resort to further the government's objectives. Once the sticks and carrots that the pervasive economic controls gave the government were taken away, the political system began to come apart. Pérez knew that his administration's economic policies would weaken the power of the state. But he miscalculated the extent to which the political system and the state had come to rely for their functioning on the government's control over the economy. Congress, the media, and the military are cases in point.

Pérez also underestimated the depth of the crises of representation and legitimacy that had beset the institutions that traditionally served as interlocutors between the government and the rest of society. Throughout his term, Pérez and his top officials spent countless hours in sessions with representatives of the traditional political parties, the *Confederacion de Trabajadores de Venezuela* (CTV—labor's main body) and FEDECAMARAS (the business sector's main body), explaining the new policies, consulting and seeking their support. It soon became evident however that these institutions were in as deep a crisis as was the government. Their relationships with the constituencies they claimed to represent were remote; their leadership was weak, divided, and out of touch with their constituencies' problems and expectations; their leaders could not commit the support of the membership to the agreements they reached with the government; and they could not provide the broader political foundation that the government needed for its reforms. Much to the contrary, it became increasingly clear that society at large deeply resented the influence of these traditional organizations. The government nonetheless continued to use them as its main interlocutors, making almost no effort at creating new channels to reach society and interact with it in a systematic and organized way.

Another example of the government's failure to discern that the old politics were out of sync with the new economics was the very limited attention it gave to the development of an effective communication strategy, an oversight with devastating repercussions. In the old scheme of things, media owners, editors, and journalists could, in effect, be "coordinated" by the government to disseminate public information. The new situation eliminated all possibility of this and left the government with no capacity to explain its policies, justify its decisions, or even clarify the misinformation spread by its opponents. Again the Pérez administration was extremely slow in recognizing this problem. It continued to communicate with the public utilizing old institutions and approaches without realizing that the conditions that made them effective in the past had ceased to exist. A completely different approach was needed but, surprisingly, Pérez did not seem bent on finding one.

A similar pattern emerged regarding attitudes towards corruption. The government grossly underestimated the extent of the nation's moral indignation and its political consequences. It assumed that the new policies would greatly diminish opportunities for corruption and that this would essentially become a problem of the past. Not only was the population unwilling to forget about the many crimes committed in previous administrations, but it was incensed by the timidity the government showed in punishing those who had been accused of abuses of power in the past. Public opinion turned against the government even more when it realized that Pérez had included in his administration individuals who had been actively involved in implementing the policies the government was now blaming for the escalation of corruption and the crisis the country was enduring. While Pérez had applied new criteria in the staffing of the main economic ministries, for most of the posts that played critical roles in the government's political or social strategy he used, with few exceptions, the same criteria that had traditionally guided the staffing of these agencies.

But in all probability, Pérez's most serious oversight was in his failure to update the old political assumptions concerning the military. Pérez introduced important changes geared to correct many of the distortions in the armed forces which had been allowed to accumulate in the past. But the government essentially took the military for granted and held to the longstanding assumption that it had relinquished its propensity to intervene in the country's political life. That assumption had been valid since democracy was reestablished in 1958, although it had not been true throughout most of Venezuela's history. It collapsed once Pérez began dismantling the state-centered model that for so many years had served to organize economic and political life. But the government took no steps toward the more comprehensive changes in mission, structure, funding, and social integration that the military needed once the old order was abandoned.

The early failures at blocking the reforms and the chaos that reigned within all political parties led Pérez to assume that he could govern alone. Pérez knew that forming a coalition with these other parties or with the newly powerful media barons would be fraught with difficulties; perhaps, it was not even necessary. However, he neglected to develop an alternative political strategy to build a base apart from the dilapidated traditional structures.

The coup attempts and the ensuing instability forced Pérez to seek the support of these traditional actors. Soon he sadly confirmed that they were neither willing nor able to help counter the instability that was threatening the survival not only of the government but of democracy itself. The political parties' capacity to be effective coalition partners, to rally support for the government or for the reforms, or to provide the votes in Congress needed to pass the political and economic program was almost nonexistent. In fact, the rifts within the parties and the public's strong antigovernment feelings made it very difficult to assemble a stable coalition that could act as an effective anchor for the country's drifting political system.

During their many years at governing in an overly comfortable situation, Venezuela's leaders had not had to cultivate the political skills needed to cope with the difficult circumstances confronting the nation. Most thus resorted to the easiest possible tack: blaming Pérez and maneuvering for his ouster. It did not matter that he had only a few months left in office or that many of the country's difficulties had little to do with who the president was. The strategy of centering the national debate on Pérez and his flaws played well in public opinion and created the political atmosphere that led to the demise of his presidency through the legal maneuverings of his enemies. Fixing on Pérez also allowed politicians to avoid having to address the country's problems. They too were applying outdated political assumptions that severely undermined any possibility of creating the consensus needed to stabilize the country.

Chapter 8
Conclusions: The Politics of Managing Economic Change

"The ancient is dying and the new has yet to be born. In this interlude, monsters are bred." So wrote Antonio Gramsci, the Italian political theorist, many years ago. Venezuela is experiencing the agonies of a country in the midst of a profound transformation. In the process, monsters have indeed been bred. The country abandoned its previous social, political, and economic system, without having yet adopted a new one. As a result, social dissent reached unprecedented levels and political conflict seriously undermined the nation's governability. Naturally, economic and social progress also suffered under such dire circumstances.

Nonetheless, many positive forces that bolster economic modernization and a strengthened democracy were set in motion at the same time. It is too early to pass judgment on which forces will come to dominate Venezuela's political and economic landscape in coming years. Venezuela's riches and other attractive characteristics (its small population, privileged location, good climate, ethnic homogeneity, three and a half decades of uninterrupted democratic rule) are indications of great promise and potential. Yet these same advantages allowed the emergence of another set of conditions that have hindered Venezuela's progress. Years of complacency led to a highly incompetent and corrupt state, appalling social inequities, a stagnant and inflationary economy, and a political system that lacked the capacity to unify society and override the veto power of the many vested interests that stand in the way of desperately needed changes.

But, even though the Venezuelan reform experience is still unfolding and its result is uncertain, it does provide some valuable insights into the nature of reform and its unexpected consequences. Moreover, while certain unique characteristics set Venezuela apart, its experience with economic and political reform is relevant not just to the rest of Latin America but to many of the countries that are making transitions simultaneously from state-centered economies to market-oriented ones and from highly centralized political systems to more open and participatory regimes.

The Link Between Economic Reforms and Political Stability

The factors at work in the Venezuelan crisis make it very difficult to establish a direct causal link between the specific nature of the economic reforms or the pace at which they were implemented and the political instability that emerged. In 1989, Venezuela was on the verge of hyperinflation and anticipated severe balance of payments and fiscal crises. Drastic shortages of food, medicines, and raw materials were emerging everywhere; the country had lost its international creditworthiness; and the state's institutional capacity to carry out public policies had been decimated. In short, there is ample reason to believe that regardless of the government's approach Venezuelans would have experienced a severe economic decline in the 1990s and the concomitant political instability. Any government assuming power in 1989 would have had to preside over a period of painful corrections of the economic errors and excesses of the past. It would also have had the task of explaining to the country that it was much poorer than what most thought and that many of the beliefs on which economic policies had been based had to be discarded.

The Pérez government had no choice but to address the macroeconomic problems with drastic and swiftly implemented reforms. Undoubtedly, this shock approach destabilized the economy and society. It also succeeded in correcting pronounced macroeconomic disequilibria in less than three years. These drastic measures were not the result of a theoretical preference for traumatic shocks; avoiding them would have required much more than the political will to choose a more gradual pace of change. They were instead the consequence of the practical impossibility of doing otherwise given the deterioration of the state apparatus. The Venezuelan experience clearly indicates the importance of including the administrative capacity of the state in any discussion of the pace at which economic reform can be implemented. The lack of institutions with even a residual capacity to function was perhaps the single most important factor in defining the nature of many of the policy decisions of the Pérez administration. Rather than fundamentalist neoliberalism, what shaped policies was the sad reality that most public agencies had ceased to exist operationally years ago.

This institutional collapse was not restricted to the public sector. Most other institutions—from universities to labor unions, from the military to political parties—on which the functioning of the political system had depended were also severely impaired. Their lack of legitimacy and responsiveness to their constituencies rendered them effectively useless as political interlocutors. The government's failure to build a more effective communication strategy compounded the problem, creating an explosive political situation. Venezuelan society was thus left totally unprepared to cope with any major change in economic policies leading to a decline in the standards of living; hence profound social and political instability were all but inevitable.

Nonetheless, the government failed to recognize that new economic policies cannot be implemented without also adjusting the leadership's assumptions about politics and political behavior. A political strategy as radically different from the past ones as its economic strategy was would not have headed off the turbulence that the nation lived through during the Pérez administration. But it could perhaps have made the process somewhat less traumatic.

The Two Phases of Economic Reform: From Issuing Decrees to Transforming Institutions

The economic reform process in Venezuela went through two clearly defined phases in terms of the instruments used to implement changes and the politics surrounding them. Most of the changes in the first phase were implemented by executive order or presidential decree; these in effect required only a cabinet meeting and the stroke of a pen. Price liberalization, the deregulation of money markets and foreign exchange transactions, trade reform, and the lifting of most restrictions on foreign investment were typical of this phase. The second phase required complex organizational transformations and, in many instances, congressional approval. Such changes include privatization, tax reform, restructuring public expenditures, developing the institutional and physical infrastructure required for a competitive export sector, developing a functioning social service delivery system, and fostering the institutional setting consistent with the new roles of the state and the private sector. Without significant support from Congress and the public bureaucracy, changes of this order proved impossible to realize.

These two phases took place amid very different political moods. During the first phase the administration not only enjoyed the confidence that public opinion usually grants newly elected governments, it was also able to capitalize on several trends that rendered opposition to the reforms quite ineffectual. Ten years of economic decay and instability during the 1980s greatly discredited the policies of those years and the politicians responsible for them in the eyes of the public. The massive shortages that emerged toward the end of the preceding administration and the near-exhaustion of foreign exchange reserves made the previous policies all but indefensible. Likewise, the main proponents of past policies were in such disrepute, they were left with no hope of mounting a credible offensive against the proposed reforms. Furthermore, the acceptability of moving away from a state-centered economy was enhanced by the radical changes taking place in Eastern

Europe and the former Soviet Union; local proponents of a larger role for the state could scarcely defend themselves in the face of international upheaval on such a scale.

Such rapid initial progress in implementing radical economic change has to be interpreted with great caution. Launching sweeping economic changes that imply a drastic break with the past is not necessarily proof of a new national consensus or a newfound effectiveness or autonomy of the state. Sweeping macroeconomic policy changes result more often from the pragmatic calculations of newly elected governments confronted with profound crisis rather than from popular consensus over a new ideology. In the subsequent phases of the reform process—as the independent executive authority has been exhausted, the administrative complexity of change reveals itself, and the patience of the population has worn thin—the typically weak ideological base of support for change begins to take its toll. Delays, distortions, bureaucratic and political imbroglios, and eventually, a degree of backsliding are normal at this stage. Also, while the initial stabilization phase affects most groups equally, the reforms of the second phase tend to be more focused in impact, dislodging entrenched interest groups. They tend to concentrate costs on specific social groups while benefits accrue to society at large, generating a skewed political reaction. The affected groups have palpable incentives to organize and obstruct changes, while the eventual beneficiaries, widely dispersed throughout the populace, are seldom even aware of the fact that reforms could benefit them.

Just as the first phase of the reforms in Venezuela benefited from the demonstration effect of the collapse of communism in Eastern Europe and the Soviet Union, the disillusionment and waning enthusiasm for economic reforms that set in a few years later was used against the second phase. The severe economic and political problems the formerly communist states faced were vaunted by the local opponents of the reforms as proof of their claim that what they pejoratively termed the technocratic, neoliberal, IMF-imposed approach was doomed.

But just as rapid initial progress in introducing policy change does not necessarily imply widespread consensus, the delays and deviations typical of the ensuing phases of the reform process should not automatically be taken as signals of the defeat of the reform initiative or the reemergence of old ways. During the normal unfolding of the second stage, the degree of resistance and unpopularity the government faces forces it to seek a broader base of political support to continue with the reforms (and even, as in the Venezuelan case, to ensure the regime's survival). It may thus cultivate a broader constituency than what it needed to get elected and launch the reforms.

Market Reforms Require an Effective State

Macroeconomic stabilization and growth are important priorities, and progress on other fronts is clearly impeded by inflation and economic stagnation. The Venezuelan experience illustrates however that without immediate reinforcement of several crucial public institutions, reduced inflation and high growth cannot hold out against the strong opposition that accompanies major economic adjustments. Upgrading the performance of public institutions after an extended period of decline is a complex process that takes a long time. Resources are rarely available to undertake needed changes across the entire spectrum of public institutions. It therefore becomes necessary to select a group of critical public institutions and focus on them.

In this regard, it should be noted that while one of the objectives of market reforms is to "get prices right," one of the prices that is often left to lag grossly behind is the salaries of senior and middle managers in the public sector. In fact, one damaging side-effect of market-oriented reforms is that they typically tend to create incentives that boost the salaries of managers in the private sector while fiscal austerity programs curb those of managers in the public sector. The lag that normally exists between the pay of private and public managers is amplified to such a degree that it makes it very difficult for the state to retain even the most civic-minded of its talented personnel. This distortion further weakens the state as it is introducing changes that are bound to weaken it even more. While across-the-board salary increases in the public sector are not advisable until the fiscal stance improves, it should be a priority to identify those institutions whose technical weakness and lack of a reliable pool of professional talent could jeopardize the entire reform program.

The implementation of grand schemes to reform the state normally takes a long time, and it is bureaucratically and politically burdensome. These ambitious plans should not be allowed to interfere with the special attention that a select group of critical institutions may require very early on in the reform process. In the Venezuelan case, the failure to upgrade the state's capacity to provide for health, personal safety, and other social services and the neglect of public information policies attuned to the special needs of the reform process made an inherently problematic situation all the more so.

The Politics of Helping the Poor

No task is more politically sensitive than attempting to upgrade the efficiency of agencies in charge of providing such public services as water, sanitation, public transportation, or such social services as health care, education, or assistance to the poor. These agencies are normally the largest public employers and therefore have very active unions that are closely connected with the political system. A strike in any of these agencies is bound to carry a heavy political cost and spark considerable turmoil. Given the instability that typically accompanies the initial stages of macroeconomic stabilization, deferring decisions expected to cause additional social and political agitation is a natural course. Restructuring the health or education ministries, for example, is so politically threatening a task that it tends to be postponed until after the waves caused by macroeconomic adjustment subside.

The Pérez administration failed to confront the unions and introduce certain badly needed changes in the crucial public agencies they
dominated. While in hindsight this proved to be a serious mistake, it
is also true that such confrontation entailed major risks for a politically
besieged government. Confronting the unions in the social sectors
would have brought on the paralysis of these institutions for an indefi-
nite period. How long could a democratic government withstand the
consequences of a strike by any essential personnel that could, in effect,
close public hospitals? How long would the population accept keeping
their children at home, at the risk of losing a school year? How long
could a government abide daily and violent marches by university
students and professors protesting budget cuts? Any of these events,
if prolonged, would spell the regime's demise. It is quite comprehensi-
ble why a government in the midst of unpopular economic reforms
would avoid taking on the unions in the public sector. Unfortunately
postponing the needed reforms in public agencies bought the Pérez
administration little support from the unions, while it created intensified opposition from all the sectors of society that had to suffer the
consequences of outrageously inefficient public services.

To address the social situation without upsetting the unions the
government created new social service delivery agencies to bypass
existing ones. Although new social programs were rapidly implemented, this solution added a new source of bureaucratic rivalry, inefficiency, and delays in responding to society's critical needs. This
partial solution also helped foster the illusion that the task of reversing
the institutional decline of the main public agencies could be further
postponed.

It would be naive to attempt to specify precise guidelines as to
the dosage of politically sensitive measures a government should take
or on the pacing of such reforms. But certain lessons should be kept
in mind. First, little else can be effectively reformed if the country
is in the grips of runaway inflation, hence the importance of rapid
macroeconomic stabilization. Yet, the Venezuelan case clearly illus-

trates that the negative political consequences of having incapacitated public service and social security agencies cannot be offset for long by progress achieved on the macroeconomic front, regardless of how substantial it may be.

Industrial Policy, Economic Reforms, and the Private Sector

The Venezuelan experience points to several generally applicable conclusions with respect to the reaction of the private sector to economic reforms. It is also clearly demonstrates the need for an industrial policy aiding export industries and the formidable constraints that limit its effectiveness.

The private sector responded vigorously to the incentives created by the new policies. However, the state's sluggishness in introducing other needed changes let undesirable corporate behaviors surface as well. Postponing financial reform allowed the financial sector to evolve in ways that jeopardized the other reforms and injected society with further political instability. The lack of an adequate legal framework to regulate the private sector permitted the kind of competitive warfare in which conglomerates engaged to take a destructive turn. This behavior added to existing political turmoil as well as contributing to increased industrial and financial concentration of ownership—a highly negative effect. Moreover, the difficulty of building effective regulatory institutions and legal instruments to monitor the newly privatized state monopolies and financial markets paves the way for future scandals and distortions. Perhaps most importantly, the failure to pass tax laws that would have increased the private sector's paltry contribution to the financing of the state furthered the deterioration of the distribution of the benefits accruing from the reforms and combined to weaken the capacity of the state to curb instability.

Another lesson of reform highlighted by the Venezuelan case is clear from the private sector's reaction to strategies aimed at increasing exports. First and foremost, a competitive exchange rate that stimulates exports is a necessary condition, but it is far from sufficient. Although it is still too early to assess the export potential of the Venezuelan private sector, many important changes will have to take place before its potential can be fully realized. These changes range from the mundane to the high profile, concerning the way in which managers are trained and recruited, the physical infrastructure needed to support export activity, the means of protecting property rights, the criteria for the appointment of ambassadors, and numerous other areas.

Competing effectively for world market shares requires much more than a stable macroeconomic environment and a competitive exchange rate.[52] In the absence of changes geared to reduce other structural impediments to the expansion of private-sector exports, the government will face continuous pressures from industrialists to devalue the bolivar. Through the undervaluation of the exchange rate, they will seek to compensate for their added costs and the effects of other deterrents to their international competitiveness.

Governments in Venezuela and in other countries that are placing their hopes on export-led economic strategies will also come under increasing pressures to actively support international expansion by specific industries and even specific firms. The pace of export expansion is likely to lag behind initial expectations, since in most countries these have tended to be overly optimistic. This optimism has, however, significantly shaped the political expectations of reform programs; export growth is one of the areas in which rapid progress is politically symbolic and economically important. Rather than disappointing expectations, governments may be lured into taking direct actions to boost exports.

Additional pressures will also arise from the example of the East Asian countries. In the mid-1990s, the rise of protectionist tendencies and the concept of "strategic" or "managed" trade in the industrialized countries, especially the United States, will also increase pressures for governments in reforming countries to follow suit.

Governments that try to refrain from engaging in an industrial policy targeted at specific industries will face practical and highly complex dilemmas. For example, the need for export leaders may conflict with attempts to implement antitrust laws. By allowing firms that are already huge by domestic standards to merge in order to achieve a size that makes them more competitive internationally, internal competition will suffer. As other governments actively seek to lure foreign firms to their soil, global competition for foreign investment will tend to create the need to promote specific sectors or niches. Under severe fiscal constraints, how should a government direct its investments in export infrastructure? What should take precedence—a new road lowering the time and costs of getting fruits to port or a technical vocational school? Shouldn't financial restrictions at home be eased to allow scarce credit to be used to ensure that exporters can fulfill their obligations to clients abroad?

These are difficult questions. In the past the Venezuelan government answered them affirmatively and selected industries on which it bestowed massive support. The results were disastrous. The answer that defenders of active industrial policies offer is that inward-oriented import substitution schemes did not provide the strong signals that a government needs to guide its actions. Export markets, however, provide the needed discipline and rapidly expose the sectors that cannot compete and which therefore should not enjoy the active support of the state.

This, of course, assumes a certain kind of state and a certain kind of private sector. In essence it assumes a state capable of independent action and private groups that are not able to impose their own will on the government. Such a state would be staffed with a well trained, stable, and knowledgeable cadre of honest and independent individuals who enjoy significant social status and can anticipate a secure retirement.

These are conditions that some East Asian countries seem to have been able to achieve. But for most other reforming countries, these are highly unrealistic assumptions for the foreseeable future. Perhaps a single piece of information can serve to illustrate the magnitude of the institutional weakness that besets these countries. In Venezuela, from 1856 to 1993, the average tenure of ministers of industry was nine months. In 1989, at the time reforms were launched, the first and second organizational levels at the ministry were staffed by newcomers with little or no government experience. They, in turn, lasted less than two years on average. The possibility of relying on the existing structure to operate was minimal. Identical conditions existed in every other agency that would have been involved in the execution of a more active industrial strategy.

State capacities to provide more effective support for the expansion of the private sector will have to be developed. But without political conditions and institutional designs that are more resistant to the self-inuring behavior that has been the norm in the past, corruption will soar much faster and much higher than exports.

The Missing Link: An Effective Communication Strategy

Nothing eases change among individuals, groups, and organizations like information and communication. The Venezuelan government ignored this fact, remaining oblivious to the need to grant public communication the same attention, resources, and seriousness as the other reforms it introduced.

Major reforms have to be explained systematically and in accessible, easily understandable terms. Many factors work against a government's efforts to explain its actions. Very often, government officials in charge of complex public policy innovations lack the ability to make their decisions intelligible to the general public. Add to this an adversarial media; a steady flow of new and unknown concepts, acronyms, and institutions; journalists who lack the training to translate technical concepts into everyday language; and the distortions introduced by opposing parties, and the result is major social confusion and political friction.

Furthermore, it is not sufficient to develop an effective communication and information strategy, it is also necessary to put in place the institutional arrangements to ensure that the strategy can be implemented with precision over an extended period of time. In many cases, existing agencies and practices are inadequate, rooted as they are in past eras when the state exercised much greater influence over the media. Major reforms create an information vacuum: the population needs to know what is happening and why, and what the consequences of the changes will be for daily life and future security.

Concomitant with the demand for information, various political and economic interests see media manipulation as a way of defending their positions or gaining new ground. Government has not only to satisfy the public's demand for information, it must simultaneously correct the distortions created by competing interests, some with considerable control over or even ownership of the media. Moreover, the public communication techniques governments usually utilize to promote their policies are not relevant to the tasks of building popular support for radical policy changes. A systematic public information campaign calls for new approaches, methods, and explanations to support economic reform strategies.

The problems a reform government faces in terms of public communication also stem from the fact that the new policies usually go against the grain of long-held beliefs, attitudes, and ideological orientations. All of the facts and messages that concern changing the approaches and policies arrived at under an older ideological framework are colored by values shaped under it. The failure of policies based on the old framework and a measure of success from the new policies are preconditions for the wider acceptance of a different ideological orientation. But the results alone are not sufficient to persuade the public. Without clear communication of strategies and goals via effective and credible leaders, the mass media, the educational system, and innovative public education efforts, a government is unlikely to generate the public support necessary to maintain the stability the new policies require.

State Autonomy and Economic Reforms

Contrary to many observers' appraisals, the principal determinant of future stability will not be the pace at which market-oriented reforms are introduced, the extent to which political power is decentralized, or the amounts spent on social policies. These are crucial factors. But, the defining element will have to do more with the state's capacity to muster the resources—political, institutional, human—necessary to exercise greater autonomy in its decisions than ever before. Technocrats dream of working with a state apparatus capable of executing "optimal" policies without major deviations and of a political context that introduces no excessive distortions into the process of formulating and executing such policies. Making such technocratic dreams a reality often means sacrificing democratic values and abiding with authoritarian proclivities—results that can, in practice, have far worse consequences than the situations they were prescribed to remedy. Technocratic omnipotence is not the reason for identifying state autonomy as the critical precondition for the implementation of economic reforms.

Instead, the need for a state capable of taking action in important areas without being subject to enormous interference from the interests of small groups emerges as a principal condition of implementing "optimal" policies to stabilize politics as well as the economy. A more autonomous state would at the same time be a reflection of a political system that has the legitimacy, the need, and the capacity to execute policies that have as their goal the long-term collective good rather than the short-term interests of powerful actors. A political system whose survival depends inordinately on its capacity to avoid conflicts with myriad special interests ends up weakening the state to the point of incapacitating it. This breeds dissatisfaction, cynicism, and the radicalization of politics.

Experience in Latin America and elsewhere shows that an authoritarian government provides no guarantee that economic policy will benefit more than a small elite at the expense of the majority of the population. The sad experience of the southern cone during the 1970s, when bureaucratic-authoritarian regimes ravaged its economies, is a powerful reminder of the consequences of authoritarian rule. In contrast, almost all of the economic reforms in Latin American countries during the 1980s that dramatically altered the relationship between the state and the dominant interest groups were adopted by democratically elected governments. Democracies, however, are also under great strain everywhere as a consequence of acute poverty, declining living standards, and generalized dissatisfaction with political institutions and political leaders. Many are also facing severe governance problems that hinder sound economic management, fueling further political turmoil.

While some understanding now exists of the conditions under which radical economic reforms are launched, still lacking is a deeper understanding of the process through which these reforms are sustained and consolidated. The Venezuelan example shows very clearly the drastic difference between the politics of launching the reforms and those of sustaining them over the long (or even the medium) term. It is crucial to gain a better understanding of the process through which a democratic government can muster the capacity to confront the powerful groups in state-centered societies that have long dominated public agencies and biased public policies.

In the case of Venezuela, reforms were essentially smuggled into the political system, and many unrelated factors converged to allow a state that had been captured and paralyzed for years to act independently of powerful interests. An economic and institutional crisis of unprecedented proportions; a daring and committed president willing to risk his popularity; a close-knit and relatively powerful group of cabinet ministers willing to challenge the interest groups that had long held the state hostage; the support of international financial institutions; the profound disrepute into which alternative courses of action and their proponents had fallen; these are some of the circumstances that accounted for the short burst of autonomy the Venezuelan state was able to command in 1989. In doubt, of course, is the permanence of these factors, since alleviating the social and economic problems that plague the country critically depends on the state's capacity to retain the necessary degree of autonomy to sustain the impulse to change. To see through the process of political and economic modernization that was set in motion, the Venezuelan political system must develop the capacity to support a state that can manage risky and complex situations and confront powerful actors.

Long-term stability in Venezuela will be regained only when additional important changes are adopted. The state has to develop the strength to modernize the institutional framework and organizational structure of the armed forces and to adapt them to the country's needs. It must acquire the capacity to effectively regulate economic life and curb the political and commercial excesses of oligopolies accustomed to having a substantial influence on government decisions. Similarly, it will have to restrain the influence of union leaders and their patrons in the political parties on the operations of public agencies, especially those in the social sector. It must also confront the mafias that have made a travesty of the country's judicial system for many years. These are not tasks for a state captured and numbed by vested interests. A working and active democracy is a powerful antidote to such numbness.

Appendix 1
Text of a Leaflet Distributed in the Streets of Caracas, February–March 1992

To the Venezuelan People

The Bolivarian Military Movement seeks, through this document, to challenge the smear campaign that has been launched against us, the Bolivarian Military, represented by our commander, Hugo Chávez Frias. In this regard, we hereby declare that: *First*: The main objective of our Movement is the recovery of the Bolivarian ideal in all its expressions and the dignity of being a soldier serving the interests of the Venezuelan nation. *Second*: To establish an emergency government comprised of the most honorable people of our country, to recover the values of the Venezuelan citizenry, and to eliminate the rampant corruption of the past thirty-four years engendered by those who, without moral or social justification, label us as criminals. *Third*: To confiscate all the assets of the politicians who have enriched themselves by plundering the national treasury and money from international loans. All these confiscated resources will be used to pay the external debt. *Fourth*: To prepare the indictments of those accused of corruption and high treason to our country in order to initiate the corresponding judicial procedures in accordance with the Constitution and the laws of the Republic, ensuring them that their individual rights, as they are established according to the rule of law, will be observed. All of this would take place under the supervision of representatives of the Inter-American Court of Human Rights. Under no circumstances do we intend to establish a dictatorship or to curtail constitutional rights, nor to violate any human rights. The only democracy that is endangered is the one associated with CAP, Ciliberto, Lusinchi, Blanca Ibanez, Vinicio Carrera, RECADI, Porfirio Valera, Avila Vivas, Henry Lopez

Sisco, Antonio Rios, David Morales Bello, Luis Herrera, Eduardo Fernandez, and Teodoro Petkoff, among others.[53] We would also like to express our condemnation of the owners of the media who, acting with complicity, misrepresented the feelings of the Venezuelan People regarding the events of February 4th. Finally, we want to make clear that our commander, Hugo Chávez Frias, as well as all the members of our movement, partake of a Bolivarian ideal. Therefore, he will never attempt to take his own life, and his physical elimination would only be possible by the criminal and corrupt hands of those who still flaunt their power. We are committed and we will never renounce our commitment and our oath to the country and to the Bolivarian way of thinking, which is why we have made the effort to be an elite battalion with an impeccable record.

> We did not lose the war but only one battle among many others still needed to realize Bolivar's dream! We still have many Chávezes! The criminals are in the government and Congress!
>
> Long live our Commander Chávez and our heroic battalion of Red Berets!

The Bolivarian Civil-Military Movement

Appendix 2
Text of a Leaflet Distributed in the Streets of Caracas, February–March 1992

For Now

On the fourth of February, the people woke up full of hopes for the insurrection by an important sector of progressive soldiers and civilians opposed to thirty-four years of democratic farce. Not knowing for certain the intentions of the rebels, we all quickly began to identify with the movement. We identified because we are fed up with so much misery, with so many lies, with so few people benefiting from the immense wealth of our country. But the happy expressions that began to appear on the faces of working people were frustrated *for now*. Nevertheless, the inexhaustible support of the people for the civilian and military insurgency has revealed the possibility of a radical change in favor of the great majority of the people. The opportunity to be free of the obstacles imposed by bureaucracy, party rule, and corruption is in our hands. . . We shall return!!! For the rescue of Bolivar's homeland, next time all of us to *Miraflores*. . .!!! Down with the forces loyal to corruption!

Acknowledgments

Joseph Tulchin and Morton Abramowitz stimulated me to write this book. Tulchin invited me to give a talk at the Woodrow Wilson Center for International Scholars in 1990 when I was still a minister in the Venezuelan government. He then sent me a transcript of my talk that made no sense and threatened to publish it. This forced me to write a more readable version, which eventually became a chapter in a book he edited. By then I had moved to the World Bank in Washington, D.C., and the first coup attempt had taken place in Venezuela. Under the auspices of the Carnegie Endowment for International Peace, I wrote an essay about the coup and its determinants. Morton Abramowitz, the president of the Endowment, encouraged me to expand it into a more comprehensive recounting of the Venezuelan experience and gave me the privilege of becoming a senior associate of the Endowment. In Mort and Joe I had incisive critics, sharp editors, and, above all, good friends.

Many people have helped with this book. I benefited from the comments of Alan Batkin, Robert Bottome, Thomas Carothers, Armeane Choksi, Imelda Cisneros, William Cline, Roberto Dañino, Rudinger Dornbush, Phillippe Erard, Judith Evans, Larry Fabian, Merilee Grindle, Peter Hakim, Jerry Helleiner, Ana Julia Jatar, Robert R. Kaufmann, Janet Kelly, Robert Klitgaard, Carmelo Lauria, Abraham Lowenthal, Fernando Martinez, Joan Nelson, Emilio Pacheco, Miguel Rodriguez, William Rogers, Pedro Rosas, Jeffrey Sachs, Francisco Sagasti, Strobe Talbott, Gustavo Tarre, Lance Taylor, and Pete Vaky.

I had the good fortune of spending many hours with Jonathan Coles, Ricardo Hausmann, Gustavo Roosen, and Gerver Torres analyzing and interpreting the experience we shared as ministers in the Venezuelan government. In these conversations they frequently offered powerful insights that have greatly influenced my own thinking and interpretations. They are great interlocutors and even better friends.

Michael O'Hare, of the Carnegie Endowment, gave generously of his time to make sure that I got all the needed assistance in the production of the book. Manuela Rangel at the World Bank was also instrumental in helping me with this project.

Adriana, Claudia, and Andrés Naim did all they could to distract me from my writing, and I am delighted that they so often succeeded. My wife, Susana, is my most important critic and supporter in this and the many other projects we share. This book is dedicated to her, again.

Notes

1. In its August 1991 report, the *International Country Risk Guide* rated Venezuela the safest investment site in Latin America and the twenty-fifth best investment site among 129 countries worldwide. Venezuela ranked higher than South Korea, Spain, Thailand, and Hong Kong, among others. *Euromoney* magazine (September 1991) raised Venezuela's ranking from sixty-fourth place in 1990 to forty-fifth in 1991 according to its analytical, credit, and market indicators. Standard and Poor's *Credit Week International* (August 5, 1991) upgraded Venezuela's Eurobond rating from BB to BB plus, while Moody's *Bond Survey* (August 1991) increased the quality of its bonds from Ba3 to Ba1. See CONAPRI, 1991.
2. See Haggard and Webb, 1992; Przeworski, 1991; Sachs, 1989a and 1989b; Nelson, 1989 and 1990; Grindle and Thomas, 1991; Kaufmann and Stallings, 1989; Haggard, 1992.
3. This account is based on Naim, 1992. For an interesting review of Venezuela's macroeconomic evolution in the twentieth century see Escobar, 1974; Hausmann, 1990a; and Frances, 1990. Unless otherwise indicated the sources for the statistics used in this book are the Central Bank of Venezuela annual reports and reports issued by OCEI, the Central Office for Statistics and Informatics. Also used were several World Bank reports (1990, 1991a, 1991c, 1991d, 1991e, 1993c, 1993d) as well as the IMF's *International Financial Statistics*.
4. Gelb and Bourguignon, 1988; Hausmann, 1991b.
5. See World Bank, 1991e.
6. See Bitar and Mejia, 1974.
7. For an elaboration of this point and its consequences in shaping many aspects of contemporary Venezuelan society see Naim and Pinango, 1974, pp. 538ff.
8. Morley, 1993; World Bank, 1991a and 1993a; Cline and Conninge, 1992.
9. See Gaceta Oficial, 1986, Presidential Decree 1717.
10. See Torres, 1993a.
11. Foreign Broadcast Information Service, *Daily Report, Latin America*. March 15, 1993, p. 53.
12. See Williamson, 1990a; Nelson, 1990.
13. In 1989, the Central Bank was sued by an individual who claimed that the bank's law obliged it to set upper and lower limits for

interest rates and that, therefore, the bank's decision to let the market determine the rates was illegal. The Supreme Court agreed and the bank had to reverse its decision. The Central Bank then defined a sufficiently wide margin between the two limits to allow supply and demand to determine interest rates. In 1992, a new Central Bank law eliminated the requirement forcing the bank to fix interest rates.

14. For an analysis of Venezuela's debt renegotiation utilizing game theory see Gueron, 1992.

15. See Palma, 1990.

16. Hausmann, 1990b and 1991a, offers a comprehensive review and analysis of the macroeconomic dynamics of this adjustment process. For the impact on the labor market and the social situation see Marquez, 1992.

17. See Morley, 1993, p. 4.

18. See Taylor, 1993.

19. The expansion of the oil, gas, and petrochemical sectors (in which foreign firms are major investors) is expected to generate about $3 billion in new investments; that of the aluminum and other metal processing operations, about $1 billion; new tourism ventures, around $1 billion; and the privatization of state-owned enterprises and utilities, about $4 billion. Furthermore, the liberalization and deregulation of the agriculture and financial services sectors is already attracting new inflows of foreign direct investment. The deregulation of the stock market has also resulted in renewed interest from international portfolio investors.

20. See Hausmann, 1991a and 1991b; Cline and Conninge, 1992; VENECONOMY, 1991; World Bank, 1993c; Torres, 1993b.

21. See Torres, 1993b.

22. Even the oil company, Petroleos de Venezuela (PDVSA), a model of efficiency internationally, fell prey to the heightened expectations brought on by the price increases of the Gulf War. The company designed a five-year, $48 billion investment program aimed at maintaining its production potential and expanding operations. Although originally approved by the executive branch, the macroeconomic implications of implementing the program had not been adequately considered. By mid-1991 and with the investment program in its preparatory stages, PDVSA was already pumping as much money into the economy each day as the rest of the public sector, creating a complex coordination problem given the Central Bank's restrictive monetary policy. Pérez replaced the president of

PDVSA and directed the new head to rationalize and limit the expansion plan.

23. From mid-1989 to mid-1991, consumer prices increased 82 percent while the wholesale price index rose 47 percent. See Cline and Conninge, 1992, p. 24

24. See Selowsky, 1990, p. 20.

25. World Bank, 1991a.

26. See Morley, 1993.

27. Conversation with author.

28. Shapiro and Taylor, 1990; Smith, 1991; Wade, 1990.

29. Krueger, 1990; World Bank, 1991d.

30. VENECONOMY, 1991b; *The Economist*, November 2, 1991.

31. Bradford and Branson, 1987; Gereffi, 1990; Wade, 1990; World Bank, 1991d.

32. World Bank, 1991a and 1993b.

33. The government nevertheless granted major exceptions to mass media companies; small- and medium-sized enterprises affiliated with a specific association, FEDEINDUSTRIA; and to a supermarket chain. These firms were allowed to swap debt for equity at deep discounts to cover the losses they (and almost all private firms) incurred due to the effects of the devaluation on their short-term commercial debts with foreign suppliers and banks which had been covered by letters of credit. The government also delayed applying trade liberalization to the automotive sector for one year, and in particular to manufacturers of auto parts. This was another example in which domestic firms were more influential than foreign companies—some of which were the subsidiaries of the largest corporations in the world—in shaping government policies.

34. CONINDUSTRIA, the business association representing manufacturing companies, sued the government unsuccessfully, requesting that it honor the foreign exchange rates contained in the letters of credit issued in 1988.

35. See International Financial Corporation, 1991 and 1992.

36. The largest and most significant of these was the hostile takeover of Banco de Venezuela by Banco Consolidado and the Latino-americana insurance and banking group. This commercial war spilled over to the state, dragging into the battle an array of public servants, politicians, and judges; the comptroller of the currency; the local equivalent of the Securities and Exchange Commission and the Internal Revenue Service; and—in the classic pattern of

Venezuelan business rivalry—journalists and assorted information gatherers.

37. See Naim, 1989a; p. 35.

38. *El Nacional*, March 9, 1991.

39. *El Universal*, February 5, 1992, as published in Ponce, 1992, p. 11; author's translation.

40. Lt. Cols. Hugo Chávez, Francisco J. Arias, Manuel Urdaneta, and Jose Ortiz.

41. Appendix 1 gives the translation of a leaflet that was widely distributed in the streets of Caracas a few days after the coup, claiming to be an official statement of the Bolivarian Military Movement and its commander, Hugo Chávez. It summarizes the group's ideas and goals. Appendix 2 gives the translated text of another flyer distributed in Caracas during the same period.

42. *El Nacional*, March 9, 1992.

43. *El Nacional*, December 2, 1992, p. D4.

44. See Sosa, 1992.

45. *El Globo*, November 28, 1992, p. 6.

46. *The New York Times*, December 6, 1992, p. L20.

47. The most extreme example of such tactics seems to have happened one night in late 1987, when a group of tanks surrounded the presidential palace and soldiers took control of the offices of the Ministry of Interior. At the time, President Jaime Lusinchi was out of the country and the minister of the interior, Simon Alberto Consalvi, was acting president. Consalvi was in his office when an officer entered to inform him that he had been sent along with the tanks to protect him. The alarmed acting president called the minister of defense at home, only to discover that the minister had no knowledge of this and ordered the officer and tanks back to their barracks. A later inquiry showed that the incident had been initiated by a call to the commander of the tank unit by a person who, after identifying himself as a senior officer and utilizing the correct secret codes, ordered the tank commander to take his unit to the presidential palace to defend it from an imminent attack. The investigation concluded that the call could not have been made by the officer under whose name the instruction had been given and that the tank commander had been tricked. While some have interpreted this incident as a failed coup and a preview of the events of 1992, others are convinced that its main purpose was to embarrass and discredit the army generals responsible for the unit, torpedoing their chances of promotion.

48. World Bank, 1992b, p. 2.
49. Employment data is from the national household survey, OCEI's *Encuesta de Hogares*, while macroeconomic data is from METROECONOMICA, December 1991.
50. The sources of these statistics are the private sector industry associations, FENAVI, CAVIDEA, CAVEDIV, CAVENEZ, AND FADAM; METROECONOMICA's report of February 1992, the Venezuelan American Chamber of Commerce economic report, and DATOS, 1991 (*National Store Audit*).
51. For further discussion of this point see Naim, 1992, p. 84.
52. See Stopford and Strange, 1991.
53. "C-A-P" are the initials of President Pérez; Lusinchi and Herrera are former presidents. Carrera and Ciliberto were cabinet members in previous administrations who were charged with corruption and fled the country. Ibanez was President Lusinchi's private secretary and later his wife. She, too, lives abroad after having been indicted by the Venezuelan courts. Valera and Lopez Sisco are former high-ranking members of DISIP, the state security police. Rios was the president of CTV, the workers' federation, and was forced to step down after being accused of corruption. Avila Vivas was governor of the Federal District (Caracas) and minister of the interior for a few weeks prior to the February 4 coup. Morales Bello was president of Congress; Fernandez was the secretary general of the Christian Democratic party; and Petkoff is a former guerrilla commander and a founder of *Movimiento al Socialismo* (MAS) for many years the third most important political party.

References

Bitar, Sergio, and Tulio Mejia. 1974. "Mas Industrializacion: Alternativa para Venezuela?" In Naim and Pinango, eds., *El Caso Venezuela*.

Bradford, Colin, and William Branson, eds. 1987. *Trade and Structural Change in Pacific Asia*. Chicago: University of Chicago Press.

Central Bank of Venezuela. Various years. *Informe Anual*. Caracas: Banco Central de Venezuela.

Cline, William R., and Jonathan Conninge. 1992. *Venezuela: Economic Strategy and Prospects*. Washington, D.C.: Inter-American Development Bank.

CONAPRI. 1991. *Venezuela Update*. Caracas: CONAPRI (National Council for Investment Promotion).

COPRE. 1993. *Un Proyecto Nacional para la Venezuela del 2000*. Caracas: COPRE (Presidential Commission on State Reform).

DATOS. 1991. *National Store Audit*. Caracas: DATOS C.A.

DATOS. 1992. *Informe Economico 1991*. Caracas: DATOS C.A.

Dornbush, Rudinger, and Sebastian Edwards, eds. 1992. *The Macroeconomics of Populism in Latin America*. Chicago: University of Chicago Press.

Escobar, Gustavo. 1974. "El Laberinto de la Economia." In Naim and Pinango, eds., *El Caso Venezuela*.

Espana, P. M., M. G. Ponce, and N. L. Luengo. 1992. *Amanecio de Golpe: El Intento de Derrocar al Presidente Pérez*. Caracas: Instituto de Investigaciones Economicas y Sociales, Universidad Catolica Andres Bello.

Foreign Broadcast Information Service. *Daily Report, Latin America*.

Frances, Antonio. 1990. *Venezuela Posible*. Caracas: Ediciones IESA.

Gaceta Oficial. 1986. *Decreto 1977*. Caracas: Imprenta Nacional.

Gelb, Alan, ed. 1988. *Oil Windfalls: Blessing or Curse?* Oxford: Oxford University Press.

Gelb, Alan, and Francois Bourguignon. 1988. "Venezuela: Absorption Without Growth." In Gelb, ed., *Oil Windfalls: Blessing or Curse?*

Gereffi, Gary, and Donald Wyman. 1990. *Manufacturing Miracles: Paths of Industrialization in Latin America and East Asia*. Princeton: Princeton University Press.

Grindle, Merilee, and John Thomas. 1991. *Public Choices and Policy Change: The Political Economy of Reform in Developing Countries.* Baltimore: The Johns Hopkins University Press.

Gueron, Eva. 1992. "Las Estructuras de Negociacion en la Renegociacion de la Deuda Externa de Venezuela." Caracas: Instituto de Estudios Politicos, Universidad Central de Venezuela. Mimeograph.

Haggard, Stephan. 1992. *Pathways from the Periphery: The Political Economy of Growth in the Newly Industrializing Countries.* Ithaca: Cornell University Press.

_____, and Steven Webb. 1992. "What Do We Know about the Political Economy of Policy Reform?" Unpublished paper.

_____, and Robert Kaufman, eds. 1992. *The Politics of Adjustment: International Constraints, Distributive Politics, and the State.* Princeton: Princeton University Press.

Hausmann, Ricardo. 1990a. *Shocks Externos y Ajuste Macroeconomico,* Caracas: Banco Central de Venezuela.

_____. 1990b. "The Big-Bang Approach to Macro Balance in Venezuela." Paper presented at the World Bank's Economic Development Institute senior policy seminar, Latin America: Facing the Challenge of Adjustment and Growth, held at IESA, Caracas.

_____. 1991a. "Adoption, Management, and Abandonment of Multiple Exchange Rate Regimes with Import Controls: The Case of Venezuela." Paper presented at the tenth Latin American meeting of the Econometric Society, Punta del Este, Uruguay.

_____. 1991b. "Dealing with Negative Oil Shocks: The Venezuelan Experience in the Eighties." Paper presented at the Conference on Temporary Trade Shocks held at St. Anthony's College, Oxford University.

Inter-American Development Bank. 1992. *Latin America in Graphs: Two Decades of Economic Trends.* Washington, D.C.: Inter-American Development Bank. Distributed by Johns Hopkins University Press.

International Financial Corporation. 1991, 1992. *Emerging Stock Markets Factbook,* Washington, D.C.: International Financial Corporation.

International Monetary Fund. Various years. *International Financial Statistics.* Washington, D.C.: International Monetary Fund.

Kaufmann, Robert, and Barbara Stallings, eds. 1989. *Debt and Democracy in Latin America.* Boulder, Colo.: Westview Press.

Kelly. Janet. 1992. "Venezuela: The Question of Inefficiency and Inequality." Paper presented at the conference, Lessons of the Venezuelan Experience. Woodrow Wilson Center and American University, Washington, D.C. October.

Krueger, Anne O. 1990. "Government Failures in Development." *Journal of Economic Perspectives*, vol. 4, no. 3 (summer).

Marquez, Gustavo. 1992. "Poverty and Social Policies in Venezuela." Paper presented at the Brookings Institution and Inter-American Dialogue conference, Poverty and Inequality in Latin America, Washington, D.C., July 1992.

Mendelson, Joanna. 1992. "The Lessons of Venezuela: Proposal Concept." Washington, D.C.: American University, Democracy Projects. Mimeograph.

METROECONOMICA. 1991. "Realidad del Sector Exportador No Tradicional." In *Hechos y Tendencias de la Economia Venzolana*. Caracas: METROECONOMICA. June.

_____. 1991, 1992. *Hechos y Tendencias de la Economia Venezolana*. Caracas: METROECONOMICA. (Monthly economic bulletin, various issues).

Morley, Samuel. 1993. "Poverty and Adjustment in Venezuela." Washington, D.C.: Inter-American Bank. Working Paper Series 124.

Naim, Moises. 1989a. "El Crecimiento de las Empresas Venezolanas: Mucha Diversificacion, Poca Organizacion." In Naim, ed., *Las Empresas Venezolanas*.

_____, ed. 1989b. *Las Empresas Venezolanas: Su Gerencia*. Caracas: Ediciones IESA.

_____. 1992. "The Launching of Radical Policy Changes: The Venezuelan Experience." In Tulchin, ed., *Venezuela in the Wake of Radical Reform*.

Naim, Moises, and Ramon Pinango. eds., 1974. *El Caso Venezuela: Una Ilusion de Armonia*. Caracas: Ediciones IESA.

Nelson, Joan, ed. 1989. *Fragile Coalitions: The Politics of Economic Adjustment*. New Brunswick, N.J.: Transaction Books.

_____, ed. 1990. *Economic Crisis and Policy Choice: The Politics of Adjustment in the Third World*. Princeton: Princeton University Press.

OCEI. Various years. *Encuesta de Hogares*. Caracas: OCEI (Central Office of Statistics and Informatics).

_____. Various years. *Encuesta Industrial*. Caracas: OCEI.

Palma, Pedro Agustin. 1990. "Una Nueva Politica Economica en Venezuela." Paper presented at the seminar, Venezuela: Development Options for the 1990s, held at the Latinamerika Institutet, Stockholm University. September.

Ponce, M. G. 1992. "El Relato y las Informaciones." In Espana, Ponce, and Luengo, *Amanecio de Golpe.*

PROMEXPORT. 1992. *Evaluacion de las Exportaciones No Tradicionales 1989-1991.* Caracas: PROMEXPORT. July. Mimeograph.

Przeworski, Adam. 1991. *Democracy and the Market: Political and Economic Reforms in Eastern Europe and Latin America.* New York: Cambridge University Press.

Sachs, Jeffrey, ed. 1989a. *Developing Country Debt and Economic Performance.* Chicago: University of Chicago Press.

_____. 1989b. "Social Conflict and Populist Policies in Latin America." NBER Working Paper 2987.

Selowsky, Marcelo. 1990. "Etapas para la Reanudacion del Crecimiento en America Latina." *Finanzas y Desarrollo*, vol. 27, no. 2 (June).

Shapiro, Helen, and Lance Taylor. 1990. "The State and Industrial Strategy." *World Development*, vol. 18, no. 6.

Smith, Stephen C. 1991. *Industrial Policy in Developing Countries: Reconsidering the Real Sources of Export-Led Growth.* Washington, D.C.: The Economic Policy Institute.

Sosa, Arturo. 1992. "El 27 de Noviembre de 1992." Mimeograph dated December 10, 1992.

Stopford, John, and Susan Strange. 1991. *Rival States, Rival Firms: Competition for World Market Shares.* Cambridge: Cambridge University Press.

Taylor, Lance, ed. 1993. *The Rocky Road to Reform.* In press.

Torres, Gerver. 1993a. "La Economia que Podemos Construir." In COPRE, *Un Proyecto Nacional.*

_____. 1993b. Comment in Gomez Emeterio, *Salidas para una Economia Petrolera.* Caracas: Cedice.

Tulchin, Joseph, ed. 1992. *Venezuela in the Wake of Radical Reform.* Boulder, Colo.: Lynne Reiner Publishers.

VENECONOMY. 1991. *Informe Mensual.* Caracas: VENECONOMY. June.

_____. 1991a. *Informe Semanal.* Caracas: VENECONOMY. Vol. 9, October 9.

Wade, Robert. 1990. *Governing the Market: Economic Theory and the Role of Government in East Asian Industrialization*. Princeton: Princeton University Press.

Williamson, John. 1990a. "What Washington Means by Policy Reform." In Williamson, ed., *Latin American Adjustment*.

Williamson, John, ed. 1990b. *Latin American Adjustment: How Much Has Happened?* Washington, D.C.: Institute for International Economics.

_____. 1991. "Development Strategy for Latin America in the 1990s." Paper presented at the Inter-American Development Bank's conference in honor of Raul Prebisch, Latin American Thought: Past, Present, and Future. Washington, D.C. November.

_____. 1993. "In Search of a Manual for Technopols." Paper presented at the conference, The Political Economy of Policy Reforms, Institute of International Economics. Washington, D.C. January.

World Bank. 1990. *Venezuela: A Review of the 1990-1993 Public Sector Investment Program*. Washington, D.C.: World Bank. Report no. 8588-VE.

_____. 1991a. *Venezuela Poverty Study: From Generalized Subsidies to Targeted Programs*. Washington, D.C.: World Bank. Report no. 9114-VE.

_____. 1991b. *Annual Review of Evaluation Results 1990*. Washington, D.C.: World Bank. Report no. 9870.

_____. 1991c. *Venezuela: Public Administration Study*. Washington, D.C.: World Bank. Report no. 8972.

_____. 1991d. *The Challenge of Development: World Development Report 1991*. New York: Oxford University Press.

_____. 1991e. *Venezuela: Industrial Sector Report* Washington, D.C.: World Bank. Report no. 9028-VE.

_____. 1992a. *Poverty Reduction Handbook*. Washington, D.C.: World Bank.

_____. 1992b. *Global Economic Prospects and the Developing Countries*. Washington, D.C.: World Bank. March.

_____. 1993a. *Poverty and Income Distribution in Latin America: The Story of the 1980s*. Washington, D.C.: World Bank. Report no. 11266-LAC.

_____. 1993b. *Venezuela 2000: Education for Growth and Social Equity*. Washington, D.C.: World Bank. Report no. 11130-VE.

——. 1993c. *Venezuela: Oil and Exchange Rates*. Washington, D.C.: World Bank. Report no. 10481-VE.

——. 1993d. *Venezuela: Structural and Macroeconomic Reforms. The New Regime*. Washington, D.C.: World Bank. Report no. 10404-VE.

Index